TWENTY TELLABLE
Tales

TWENTY TELLABLE Tales

Audience Participation Folktales for the Beginning Storyteller

BY

MARGARET READ MACDONALD

Drawings by Roxane Murphy

THE H. W. WILSON COMPANY

1986

SECOND PRINTING 1987
THIRD PRINTING 1989

Library of Congress Cataloging-in-Publication Data
MacDonald, Margaret Read.
      Twenty tellable tales.
      Includes bibliographies.
      1. Elementary school libraries — Activity programs.
2. Storytelling.   3. Tales.   1. Title.
Z675.S3M16   1986   027.8'222   85-26565
ISBN 0-8242-0719-X

For two storytellers:

Bob Polishuk,
   who taught me how to tell,
Spencer Shaw,
   who taught me how to teach.

      and for two listeners:
      Jenny, who listens and retells

      Julie, who listens and draws.
      Here is her "Little Rooster."

PREFACE

In the spring of 1983 I spoke to a group of school librarians in Seattle. One of my former storytelling students was there. Although she had been a promising beginning teller, she told me she no longer had time in her career to learn new stories and continue telling. It was just that storytelling was so difficult, so time consuming. This was a problem I had heard many times before.

I decided there must be a way to make storytelling easier. If the activity was to fit into the busy schedules of school librarians and teachers it must take less preparation time. I called the Washington Library Media Association and offered a workshop for the fall conference. The title? "How to Learn a Story in One Hour." From that workshop the idea for this book was born. Then, in the winter quarter of 1984 I was fortunate to teach a storytelling class for practicing school librarians and teachers, which gave me the opportunity to test and shape my methods. Since then, I have found much enthusiasm among teachers and librarians for these somewhat unusual techniques.

In this book you will find instructions for selecting, shaping, learning, and telling a tale; a set of twenty tales designed for easy learning and effective oral performance; notes suggesting effective ways to tell each tale; notes on the origins of each tale; selective bibliographies to start you on your way to further study or other tales; comments on audience participation and performance style in other cultures; and a discussion of how to move a tale from the medium of oral performance to that of the printed page.

The twenty tales I have chosen are all short and employ repetition in their storylines. Most of the tales contain chants, songs, or refrains. These factors—brevity, repetition, memorable refrains—should make the tales easy to learn. However, the transcripts are offered purely as suggestions; if my style does not feel right to you, locate other texts for these tales or work out your own tellings.

I have set the tales in an "ethnopoetic" format in order to make them easier to read aloud. My aim is to allow the reader to adopt an oral style as quickly as possible. The tales we usually encounter in children's collections have often followed a strained path from oral storyteller, to anthropologist, to anthropological journal, to author of children's books, to printed page. It is often difficult for the beginning teller to sense just how this printed short story can be made alive through oral presentation. My "ethnopoetic" format simply consists of a restructuring of sentences into shorter units of spoken phrases, coupled with a few simple reading cues marking emphasis.

Dennis Tedlock, Professor of anthropology and religion at Boston University, and others have been experimenting with such formats in an attempt to help the reader reconstruct the speech patterns of the speaker. Tedlock's collection of Zuni tales *Finding the Center* is a successful example of this technique. The journal *Alcheringa Ethnopoetics* dealt also with this problem of transferring oral text to printed page.

It seemed to me that it might be useful to transcribe my tales as they are actually told and set them down for other tellers. These tales have been reworking themselves for years and now hold very little similarity to the printed sources from which I first took them. They have moved a long way from the printed page back toward an oral style. Seven of the tales were in fact taken from other tellers and learned aurally before I consulted a printed text.

Teachers find that children who have heard these tales are also eager to read them to themselves. The oral nature of the language and the ethnopoetic format make the tales easy to read. I think your children will enjoy reading these tales as well as hearing them.

I selected these particular tales from my repertoire because they promised easy success for the beginning storyteller. However, when I examined the tales more carefully I realized that something interesting had happened to each tale since I started telling it. Each has grown over the years into an audience participation tale. Since audience participation requires a storyteller who is at ease with the audience, I hesitate to suggest that a beginning teller tackle that technique. It is true, however, that as soon as you begin to relax with your audience you will find that the children seem to want to chime in on the repetitive refrains and phrases. If you feel comfortable letting your storytelling take this form, just relax and encourage your audience to take part in the telling. Storytelling in this form takes on some of the features of group drama. It can provide a rewarding shared experience for both teller and audience.

Suggestions for using these tales as audience participation are given in the "Notes" for each tale. In general, to get an audience to join in on a refrain, you must pause, gather the group with your eyes, and let them know by an air of expectation that you want *them* to help you with what comes next. Nod encouragement to those who do chime in and soon the whole group will be participating. It usually is not necessary to ask them "Do you want to help me say the chant?" If a group does not readily join in, I simply change my style and tell without the participatory approaches. Some groups are more comfortable listening quietly.

I do not mean to suggest that the participatory approach to storytelling is the only, or even the preferred, method of storytelling. Many tales must be told quietly and are to be enjoyed in a silent, receptive mood. These tales work beautifully as simple tellings without using audience participation techniques. Try them both ways and choose the telling techniques that feel best to you. Audience participation simply adds variety and a different kind of joy to the storytime.

Most of all, have fun! These tales have delighted both children and adults for centuries. Tell them and pass them on.

ACKNOWLEDGMENTS

Thanks to all my students, but especially to: Jan Bertschi, Karen Bawden, Mary Lou Burns, Fay Dawson, Jeanie Garrioch, Edwina Hampton, Lee Henderson, Mae Krǎvik, Tom Nielsen, and Billie Noe.

Thanks to Mariko Martin for help with the Japanese tales, to Rosemarie Peterson for German translation, and to my father, Murray Read for retelling the stories of Parley Garfield Read for me.

My views on the social identity of the storyteller are influenced by Robert J. Adams and his excellent study "The Social Identity of a Japanese Storyteller" (Ph.D. dissertation, Indiana University, 1972).

I am grateful to my editors, Bruce Carrick and Ellen Lehman, for saying no at the right times and yes when it was important.

CONTENTS

A NOTE TO THE TEACHER
OF STORYTELLING

The techniques outlined in this book have proved effective for use with students who have a built-in audience to whom the tales may be told. School librarians are the ideal candidates, but primary-grade teachers have also had success with these suggestions.

In the beginning, I give my students no instruction about how to learn or perform a tale. In fact, I ask them not to begin reading storytelling texts until after the second class. Instead, I teach the entire class a simple, repetitive story that usually includes audience participation. As I perform the story for the class, I encourage them to join in where appropriate, and immediately, they become involved. I then begin telling the story a second time, asking them to tell with me as best they can. Next, we pass the tale around the room, each student telling a segment in turn. I then distribute the tale text transcribed from my own telling, and armed with this, the students go home to tell the tale as many times as possible before the next class.

Since the students have not yet been told that storytelling is a difficult and demanding art form, they just go back to their schools and start telling this first story without worry about style and technique. Later, when they have begun to identify themselves as "storytellers," we will begin to refine their individual styles.

One exciting result of a teaching technique in which everyone learns the same story is the lack of any sense of story ownership. Tales are seen as artistic pieces that anyone can use, just as anyone can recite a poem or read aloud a short story.

I choose short, repetitive tales that I know will delight audiences and are easily learned. The audience participation technique gives beginning tellers the immediate feedback that is so vital in encouraging them to pour effort into the more difficult stages of storytelling training to come. By making the audience a partner in the telling, the fear of performance is lessened and the teller soon relaxes and begins to enjoy. Although effective use of audience participation would seem to require a skilled teller, the reinforcement gained from this technique is positive even in the hands of the beginner.

The students find this method of learning fairly painless, telling me that they know the story by the time they leave our first class, and need only minimal preparation before beginning to tell. I stress the importance of repeated performance with my students. They are to refine the tale through many performances, rather than through hours of preliminary practice. I require that every student learn and perform at least one new tale each week, but most classes demand more than one tale per week, because their own students are clamoring for more!

By the third week of class, my students have already begun to form reputations in their own schools as storytellers. As word quickly spreads among the children, my students find their newfound talents in great demand. Once the identity of "storyteller" has been assumed by a student, the important barrier between simply taking a class in storytelling and becoming a lifelong storyteller has been crossed.

PART I: TALES

A WHALE OF A TALE

Once in the Far North
there lived a little boy who was *always* hungry.

He lived with his grandmother
in an igloo.

One day the old woman called the little boy and said:
    "There's not a scrap of blubber left in the igloo.
    You'll have to go out and find some food for
       yourself."

By the light of the midnight sun
the little boy went out
and walked along the shore.

1

Suddenly he saw
lying on the ice
a *tom codfish*.

Quickly
the boy *grabbed* the tom codfish by the tail with one
    hand . . .
pulled off its head with other hand . . .
and *glump!*
He swallowed the codfish down.

> "That was *good*," said the little boy.
> "But do you know something? . . .
> I'm *still* hungry."

He went on down the shore
And he saw
lying on the ice
a *seal*.

Quickly
he grabbed the seal by the tail with one hand . . .
pulled off its head with the other hand . . .
and *glump!*
He swallowed the seal down.

> "Now *that* was good," said the little boy.
> "But do you know something?
> I'm *still hungry*."

He went on down the shore.

And soon he saw
lying on the ice
an *Oogluk*.

That is a *giant* kind of seal.

Quickly
he grabbed the Oogluk by the tail with one hand...
he pulled off its head with the other hand...
and *glump!*
He swallowed the Oogluk down.

> "That was *good!*" said the little boy.
> "But do you know something?...
> *I'm still hungry.*"

He went on down the shore
and he saw
lying on the ice...
a *walrus!*

Quickly
he grabbed the walrus by the tail with one hand...
he pulled off its head with the other hand...
and *glump!*
He swallowed the walrus down.

> "Oh that was *good,*" said the little boy.
> *"But do you know something?...
> I'm still hungry."*

He went on down the shore.
And he saw lying on the ice
one *great...white...whale!*

The little boy grabbed the whale by the tail with one
    hand...
and pulled off its head with the other hand...
and *glump! glump! glump!*
He swallowed the whale down.

      "That was *good*," said the little boy.
      "And do you know?...
      I...think...I...am...finally
      f-u-l-l."

He started to walk home.

But he was thirsty.
He came to a pond
and started to drink.
He drank and drank and drank...
He drank up the *whole* pond.

Then he sang a little song
to tell the whole wide wet world
how *happy* he was.

But when he came to the igloo
his *head* wouldn't even go through the door
he'd gotten SO fat.

A WHALE OF A TALE

"I can't get in the door!"
he called to the old lady inside.

"Then come in the *window*,"
said the old woman.

"The *window* is smaller than the *door*,"
thought the little boy.
"But if *she says so*
I can but try."

The little boy went around
and as if by *magic*
his head did go right through that window.
But his *shoulders* wouldn't go.

"No I can't get through the window!"

"Then you'll have to come in the *smoke hole*,"
said the old woman.

"The *smoke hole?*
Why that's even smaller than the *window*."

"But if she says so
I can but try."

The little boy went around
and as if by magic
his head *and* his shoulders
went right through that *tiny* smoke hole.

But his *tummy* wouldn't go.

"I can't get through the smoke hole either."

"Then you'll have to come in
through the *eye* of my *needle*,"
said the old woman.

She held out her *needle*...
and...
in he tumbled
onto the floor of the igloo!

"LOOK OUT FOR THE SEAL OIL LAMP!"
cried the old woman.

But it was *too late*.

The little boy stumbled.
He fell against the seal oil lamp...
and...POP!

When the old woman woke up
she was lying on the ice
outside the igloo.

The igloo was gone.

The seal oil lamp was gone.

The little boy was gone.

6

And where they had been
there was a *pond* of water.

And in the pond of water
swimming slowly round and round...
was a tom codfish.
A seal.
An Oogluk.
A walrus.
and a *great...white...whale.*

And that
is a *whale* of a *tale.*

NOTES ON TELLING

I learned this story from the delightful telling by Patricia Stegall in the film "There's Something About a Story." You should be able to learn it almost painlessly by viewing the film once or twice.

I encourage audience participation in this story by addressing the little boy's repeated question "Do you know something?" to the audience. Most children quickly chime in with his "I'm *still hungry.*" If you wish the group to join you in his response, address the question squarely to the audience, pause, and then nod encouragement to those who begin to mouth the response. Some audiences will join in immediately. Others never pick it up. I encourage them with a nod if they start to join in, but I do not stop and ask them to join in. The tale works fine with or without response.

Primary classes love this tale and often ask to have it repeated. Children below second grade, however, sometimes misunderstand the ending. Only a few understand that the little boy exploded. Others think the whale may have eaten him. I like the pacing of this tale's ending and so have kept it as it is, rather than rewording it to make it more self-explanatory. After the tale ends I explain to the audience that the little boy had eaten so much that he just exploded when he fell against that seal-oil lamp.

Although I dislike prefacing tales with lengthy background information, I do sometimes mention a few facts about Eskimo life before beginning this tale: the use of bone needles, seal-oil lamps, blubber, and igloos.

COMPARATIVE NOTES

A charming library telling of this tale may be seen in the film "There's Something About a Story." This telling is probably taken from Jean Cothran's *The Magic Calabash: Folk Tales from America's Islands and Alaska.* Cothran cites as source *Igloo Tales* by Edward L. Keithahn (p. 19). Keithahn's tales were collected on the Seward Peninsula while he was teaching there. He thanks the children of Shishmaref, Alaska. The book has been illustrated by Shishmaref Eskimo George Aden Ahgupuk.

Another version of this tale is available on a recording, *Alaskan Eskimo Songs and Stories: Compiled and Recorded by Lorraine Donoghue Koranda.* The tale is told on this recording by Maggie Lind of Bethel, Alaska. In the booklet that accompanies the album, Koranda states that the tale is widely known.

In Lind's version the little boy drinks the ocean dry. When he bursts, his grandmother gets into one of the ships he has swallowed and escapes. Koranda mentions other versions of the story in which the little boy swallows dogs and hunters who become so hot in his stomach that they come out hairless.

Notation for the song the little boy sings before eating each fish is given in the booklet accompanying Koranda's record. Lind's recorded telling includes the song.

MacDonald's *Storyteller's Sourcebook* indexes this tale as Motif X1723 *Lies about swallowing* and D1181.1 *Magic needle.*

A WHALE OF A TALE

Tales of magic stomachs capable of swallowing everything in sight are common throughout folk literature. For a few examples, see MacDonald or Thompson Z33.2 *Glutton swallows everyone it meets*; K952 *Animal or monster killed from within*; F912 *Victim kills swallower from within*; F601.2 *Extraordinary companions (one of them is a swallower)*. See also comparative notes in this book for "Sody Sallyrytus," and "The Little Rooster and the Turkish Sultan."

The reverse magic sequence, in which the little boy fits progressively more easily into a door, window, smoke hole, and needle, is unusual.

The English pun "a whale of a tale" was used by Cothran as the title of her version of the story. It works even better moved to the tale's end as a punch line.

Keithahn's version has the boy trying to enter the igloo through a ventilator. Cothran uses the more ethnic-sounding "smoke hole."

In *Noodles, Nitwits and Numskulls* (p. 87) Maria Leach gives a tale "Through the Needle's Eye" in which an Eskimo boy sings a song while walking along the shore and stuffing his shirt full of seaweed for his grandmother and himself to eat. He enters the house through the eye of her needle, at which point the tale ends. Leach took her tale from *The Eskimo of Siberia*, Publication of the Jessup North Pacific Expedition (p. 420), collected by Waldemar Bogoras.

9

COYOTE'S CRYING SONG

One day Little Dove was gathering kwakwi seed for
   the winter.
She would pick the kwakwi grass
And she would rub it between her little feet to get
   the seeds out.
But the kwakwi grass was very sharp.
While she was rubbing
she cut her foot on the sharp grass.

Little Dove began to cry:
        "Hoo hoo hooo
        Hoo hoo hooo
        Hoo hoo hoo hoo hoooo
        Hoo hoo hoooo."

And she began to blow on her cut foot.

Just then Coyote came loping across the desert.

10

COYOTE'S CRYING SONG

"Oh Little Dove!
What is that lovely *song* you are singing?"

"I wasn't singing a song.
I cut my foot and I was crying."

"It sounded like a song to me.
Don't tell me I don't know a song when
    I hear one!
Sing it again, Little Dove.
I want to learn your song."

"But I was only crying."

"Little Dove you had better
Sing that song again.
Or I will have to
EAT YOU UP."

So Little Dove began to cry again:
    "Hoo hoo hooo
    Hoo hoo hooo
    Hoo hoo hoo hoo hoooo
    Hoo hoo hoooo."

"Thank you, Little Dove.
I think I have learned the song,"
said Coyote.

And he loped off across the desert.

"Hoo Hoo Hooo   [in low, huffy coyote voice]
Hoo Hoo Hooo
Hoo Hoo Hoo Hoo Hoooo
Hoo Hoo Hooo...Ooopps!"

And not looking where he was going
Coyote tripped and fell down.
When he got up
he had forgotten the song.

"What was that song?
I've dropped my song.
How did it go?
Hu...? Ho...? Huh...?
I'll have to go back and ask Little Dove
    to sing again."

Coyote went back to where Little Dove was gathering
   her kwakwi seed.

"Little Dove
Will you sing that song again for me?"

"I wasn't singing
I was *crying.*"

"I know a *song* when I hear one.
You sing it again.
Or I will have to
EAT YOU UP."

12

Little Dove began to cry:
    "Hoo hoo hooo
    Hoo hoo hooo
    Hoo hoo hoo hoo hoooo
    Hoo hoo hoooo."

    "Thank you Little Dove
    Now I have it!"

Coyote loped off across the desert.

    "Hoo Hoo Hooo
    Hoo Hoo Hooo
    Hoo Hoo Hoo Hoo Hoooo
    Hoo Hoo Hooo...whoops!"

Coyote tripped and fell.

    "I've forgotten my song!
    How did that go?
    Huu... haa... huuh...?
    I'll have to go back and ask Little Dove."

    "Little Dove
    Would you sing that song again for me?"

    "I wasn't singing
    I was *crying*."

    "I know a *song* when I hear it.
    Sing that again

Or I will have to
EAT YOU UP."

"All right then...
Hoo hoo hooo
Hoo hoo hooo
Hoo hoo hoo hoo hoooo
Hoo hoo hoooo."

"I know it *now*.
Thank you Little Dove."

Coyote loped off across the desert.

*"Hoo Hoo Hooo
Hoo Hoo Hooo
Hoo Hoo Hoo Hoo Hoooo
Hoo Hoo Hoooo..."*

Meanwhile
Little Dove thought:
"I had better leave this place.
That foolish Coyote will forget his song and
come back.
He might really
EAT ME UP!"

Little Dove found a rock that was shaped like a dove.
She *covered* it over with kwakwi grass.
She painted two little eyes on the rock.

14

Then Little Dove gathered up her kwakwi seeds
and went home.

Coyote was loping happily across the desert.

> *"Hoo Hoo Hooo*
> *Hoo Hoo Hooo*
> *Hoo Hoo Hoo Hoo Hoooo*
> *Hoo Hoo Hooo...ooops!"*

> "No. No!
> I fell down again.
> I have dropped that slippery song.
> How did it go?
> Ho... Hu... Ha...?
> I will have to go back and ask Little Dove."

When Coyote went back
He saw the rock Little Dove had fixed.

> "Little Dove
> Sing that song for me again."

But *this* "Little Dove" was only a *rock*
and the rock could not *answer*.

> "Little Dove
> Sing that *song*.
>
> Little Dove
> If you don't sing that song

15

I will have to
EAT YOU UP."

The rock did not answer.
So Coyote opened his huge jaws...
and *snapped.*

Ohhhhhhhhhhh

All of his *teeth* fell out of his head.

> "Hoo hoo hooo
> Hoo hoo hooo
> Hoo hoo hoo hoo hoooo
> Hoo hoo hoooo."

Coyote began to *cryyyyy.*

Just then *crow* flew down.

> "Oh Coyote
> What a beautiful song you are singing.
> Could you teach it to *me?*"

> "How foolish the crows are" said Coyote.
> "They can't tell *singing*
> from *crying.*

> *Hooooooooo...*"

16

NOTES ON TELLING

The amount of audience involvement in this tale will depend on the age level of your group. When working with pre-schoolers, I involve them immediately in this story by asking them to help Little Dove rub her kwakwi grass. Both pre-school and primary children love to help Little Dove and Coyote sing their songs.

After Little Dove sings her crying song the first time, ask your audience to help her sing as you repeat the song. I hold my own hand up as if blowing on a cut as I sing Little Dove's song.

Coyote sings his song strongly in a low, huffy, monotone coyote voice. He should lope proudly across the desert, huffing and puffing as he sings. I suggest his swaggering jog by swinging my arms just slightly while I huff his "Hoo hoo hoooo's." I break Coyote's last "Hoooo" with a feigned trip, showing by my action just what happens.

When Coyote tries to remember his song, he may pretend to be asking the audience how that song went, but cut ahead to the next line quickly or they will tell him.

When Little Dove fixes the rock to look like a dove, take your time with the imagery. I use my hands to show her action, covering over the rock with kwakwi grass and painting the eyes.

You can use your arms or open jaws to show how Coyote's teeth snapped on the rock.

Coyote's last crying song should be very similar in tone to Little Dove's opening song. He is crying himself now, not singing.

Hoo Hoo Hoo Hoo Hoo Hoo Hoo Hoo Hoo Hoo Hoo-o

COMPARATIVE NOTES

Inspiration for this tale is drawn mainly from Harold Courlander's version in *People of the Short Blue Corn: Tales and Legends of the Hopi Indians* (p. 82-85).

In other variants of this tale Coyote threatens a locust. Locust leaves his shell behind on a rock and Coyote bites the rock. This version appears in *Pueblo Stories* by Marguerite and Edward Dolch (p. 67-77). Harold Courlander's *Ride with the Sun: An Anthology of Folk Tales and Stories from the United Nations* (p. 234-237) contains a Nicaraguan version in which Coyote threatens a cicada if it will not stop singing.

In Jane Louise Curry's *Down from the Lonely Mountain: California Indian Tales* (p. 104-110), Coyote threatens hare and eventually proposes a heat-endurance contest for possession of the song. Moritz Jagendorf's *Noodlehead Stories from around the World* (p. 274-277) does not have a forgetful coyote but does show Coyote threatening a baby turtle unless it sings. Turtle escapes by begging not to be thrown into the water (K581.1). Amabel Williams-Ellis includes this tale in her *Round the World Fairy Tales* (p. 231-232).

Elsie Clews Parson recorded several variants of this tale in "Pueblo-Indian Folk-Tales, Probably of Spanish Provenience" (*Journal of American Folk-Lore*, Vol. XXXI, April-June 1918). She gives a variant of Coyote and Locust (p. 222-225) and another variant that pits Coyote against a family of meadow larks (p. 226-227).

In the meadow lark version Coyote is trying to carry water in his mouth. He spills it every time he attempts to exclaim or sing and has to go back for more water.

Coyote's preoccupation with songs seems constant. An unrelated tale about spider and her children opens with Coyote trying to learn spider's song (Parsons, p. 227-229). Another tale shows six coyotes hanging by each other's tails in a chain, attempting to steal a song from dancers below (p. 233-235).

In the *Journal of American Folk-Lore* (Vol. XXXIII, January-March 1920, "Spanish Tales from Laguna and Zuñi,

New Mexico" by Elsie Clews Parsons and Franz Boas (p. 47-48) we find another variant. Here the coyote is a female, carrying water in her mouth to her young. She exclaims at Quail's song and loses the water. Coyote threatens Quail's stuffed image four times before biting.

Dennis Tedlock gives a variant very close to the Courlander Hopi version in his *Finding the Center: Narrative Poetry of the Zuni Indians*. In "Coyote and Junco" (recorded in Zuni, with an ethnopoetic adaptation in English, p. 75-84), a junco is forced to teach Coyote her winnowing song. Coyote stumbles and forgets the song, and threatens four times before biting.

"Coyote's Crying Song" includes Thompson motif K525 *Escape by use of substituted object* and G555 *Rescue from ogre by means of singing*. It is related to K551.3.2.1 *Respite from death while one sings song*. This tale is also related to J2671 *The forgetful fool* and D2004.5 *Forgetting by stumbling*. MacDonald's *Storyteller's Sourcebook* indexes this tale under G555.1.2★ and K525.1.4★. The tale is related to Aarne-Thompson Type 1687 *The Forgotten Word. The fool as he falls into hole forgets the word which he is to remember* and Type 1204 *Fool keeps repeating his instructions so as to remember them.*

COYOTE'S RAIN SONG

Coyote stood on the hill overlooking prairie dog town.
Coyote thought:
> "I am hungry for prairie dog meat.
> I'll make it *rain*.
> I'll make it rain on prairie dog town.
> I'll wash those prairie dogs
> *right out of their holes*."

Coyote began to chant
his magic *rain-making song*.

> "Rain! Dark Cloud, Rain Cloud.
> Rain on Prairie Dog Town.
> Rain!
> Rain!
> Rain!
> Rain!"

20

Coyote chanted his song *four times*.
Four is the magic number.

First time:
      "Rain! Dark Cloud, Rain Cloud.
      Rain on Prairie Dog Town.
      Rain!
      Rain!
      Rain!
      Rain!"

Second time:
      "Rain! Dark Cloud, Rain Cloud.
      Rain on Prairie Dog Town.
      Rain!
      Rain!
      Rain!
      Rain!"

Third time:
      "Rain! Dark Cloud, Rain Cloud.
      Rain on Prairie Dog Town.
      Rain!
      Rain!
      Rain!
      Rain!"

Fourth time is the *magic* time:
      "Rain! Dark Cloud, Rain Cloud.
      Rain on Prairie Dog Town.
      RAIN!
      RAIN!

RAIN!
RAIN!"

It began to rain.

It rained to the *north* of prairie dog town.
It rained to the *south* of prairie dog town.
It rained to the *east* of prairie dog town.
It rained to the *west* of prairie dog town.

But it did *not* rain
on prairie dog town.

The prairie dogs laughed at Coyote
slinking away in the rain.

"Your song is no *good*, Coyote..."

"Your song is no *good*...."

NOTES ON TELLING

This brief story should be easy to learn. I like to let the children join me in Coyote's chants. I have used this in pre-school storytimes very successfully. It worked well even with the two and a half year old groups. Participation is often the key to success when attempting storytelling with such young children. Of course, older kids love this story too.

After I perform Coyote's chant the first time, I invite the group to try performing his chant with me. When we have practiced it once or twice, I continue with the story and they join in on each of Coyote's four chants. I pause before the fourth magic chant and gather the force of the group together for a very strong performance of this last chant.

I clap during the chant, stressing the chant on the underlined words:

Rain Dark Cloud *Rain* Cloud.

Rain on Prairie Dog *Town.*

The texts available to us give no musical notation or instructions for movement with this tale. Use those I have invented or try your own.

With firm beat

Rain! dark cloud, rain cloud. Rain on prair-ie dog town.

COMPARATIVE NOTES

A brief text of this tale will be found in Natalia Belting's *Our Fathers Had Powerful Songs*. Belting lists the tale as Apache but cites no source.

The Thompson motif D2143.1 *Rain produced by magic* has worldwide distribution. Thompson cites Irish, Icelandic, Jewish, Indian, Chinese, Korean, Philippine, Eskimo, and African variants.

Coyote's ability to sing down the elements appears in other tales as well. In *As One Is So One Sees: Stories, Poems and Epigrams* (Floating Eagle Feather, editor), Coyote and Badger sing for snow. *Coyote Stories of the Navajo People* by Robert A. Roessel, Jr. and Dillon Platero (p. 1-4) finds Coyote calling down rain until he floats away on the flood.

In a more lengthy tale in which Coyote plays dead to entice prairie dogs near, Coyote calls down rain on prairie dogs as an opening motif. See Barre Toelken's "'Pretty Language' of Yellowman" (*Folklore Genres*, edited by Dan Ben-Amos, p. 145-170) for an interesting variant and a discussion of performance and cultural relevance. The tale also appears in Elsie Clews Parsons' "Navaho Folk Tales" (*Journal of American Folk-Lore* XXXVI, October-December 1923, p. 371-372) and in *Navaho Texts* (p. 20-25), edited by Edward Sapir and Harry Hojier.

LITTLE CRAB AND HIS MAGIC EYES

Once upon a time
there was a little crab
who had *magic eyes*.

He could make his eyes
pop out of his head
and go flying out over the ocean...
and then fly back and pop into his head again.

He would sit along the seashore
and play his eye sailing game.

He would call:
    "Little Eyes...
    Little Eyes...
    Sail *out*
    Over the *Deep Blue Sea*."

And Little Crab's eyes would
POP out of his head
and *sail out* over the Deep Blue Sea.

Then he would call:
    "Little Eyes...
    Little Eyes...
    Sail *back*
    Over the Deep Blue Sea."

And his eyes would *sail* back and
POP into his head again.

It was a good game.

Little Crab's eyes could look down into the blue sea.
They could see the seaweed...
the coral reef...
the fish swimming about...
It was fun!

One day when Little Crab was playing his eye sailing
   game along came Jaguar.

Jaguar said:
    "Little Crab
    What are you doing?"

    "I'm playing my eye sailing game.
    I can make my eyes *sail* out
      over the deep blue sea
    and come back again!"

25

"Little Crab, let me see you do it.
Do it for *me* Little Crab."

"All right!" said Little Crab.
And Little Crab began to play his game.
He called:
    "Little Eyes...
    Little Eyes...
    Sail *out*
    Over the *Deep Blue Sea.*

And Little Crab's eyes
POPPED out of his head
and *sailed* out over the Deep Blue Sea.

Then he called:
    "Little Eyes...
    Little Eyes...
    Sail *back*
    Over the Deep Blue Sea."

And his eyes *sailed* back
and POPPED into his head again.

    "Oooooohhhh
    that looks like *fun*,"
    said Jaguar.
    "Little Crab,
    could you make *my* eyes go sailing?"

LITTLE CRAB AND HIS MAGIC EYES

"I *could*,"
said Little Crab
"But I'm not *going* to.
It's *too* dangerous."

Out in the Deep Blue Sea
there lives a big
Oonkaloonka fish.
And the *Oonkaloonka* fish
might *swallow* your eyes.

"I'm not afraid of any old *fish*,"
said Jaguar.
"You make my eyes go *sailing*.
You make my eyes go sailing or
You'll be s-o-r-r-y."

So Little Crab said, "All right!"
He began to call:
"Jaguar's Eyes...
Jaguar's Eyes...
Sail out
Over the *deep blue sea*."

And Jaguar's eyes
POPPED out of his head
and *sailed* out
over the Deep Blue Sea.

Then Little Crab called
"Jaguar's Eyes...

Jaguar's Eye's...
Sail back
Over the Deep Blue Sea."

And Jaguar's eyes *sailed* back
and POPPED into his head again.

"*Oooooohhhhhh!*
That was *wonderful!*"
said Jaguar.
"I could see the fish
and the coral reefs
and *everything!*"

"DO IT AGAIN!
DO IT AGAIN! LITTLE CRAB!"

"No. It's *too* dangerous.
That *Ooonkaloonka* fish
might *swallow your eyes.*"

"I'm not afraid of any old *fish!*
You make my eyes go *sailing* again.
You make my eyes go sailing or
You'll be s-o-r-r-y."

So Little Crab said:
  "All right. *All right.*

Jaguar's Eyes...
Jaguar's Eyes...
Sail *out*
Over the Deep Blue Sea."

Jaguar's eyes
POPPED out of his head
and sailed out over the Deep Blue Sea.

Then Little Crab called:
    "Jaguar's Eyes...
    Jaguar's Eyes...
    Sail back
    Over the Deep Blue Sea."

But just then up
came the *Ooonkaloonka* fish
and *swallowed* Jaguar's eyes.

    "Oh Little Crab!
    It all went black!
    I can't see!"

    "Bring them BACK!
    Bring back my EYES!"

    "It's *too* late,"
    said Little Crab.
    "That Oonkaloonka fish has *swallowed*
    your eyes."

"Little Crab
You make my eyes come back
or you'll be SORRY!"

But Little Crab had backed under a rock
and Jaguar could not find him.

Jaguar began to *moan* and *groan*.

Just then down flew Vulture.

"Jaguar,
Why are you crying?"
said Vulture.

"I'm crying because Little Crab took my *eyes* away.
And he will not bring them back.
I can see nothing at all."

"What would you do if I brought you some
    new eyes?"
asked Vulture.

"I would do *anything*.
From now on
whenever I kill an animal
I will leave the carcass,
the bones, and some of the meat
for the Vulture family."

30

"Very well,"
said Vulture.

And Vulture flew away.
Soon he flew back
with two *bright blue berries*.

Jaguar popped
them into his eyes.
And he could see as well as ever!

Everything was bright and blue and shiny.

"I can SEE!
I can SEE!!"
said Jaguar.

"Thank you, Vulture.
From now on
Whenever I or any member of the Jaguar family
    kill an animal
We will leave the carcass,
the bones, and some of the meat
for the Vulture family."

And so it is to this day.

Then Jaguar called:
"Little Crab,
I am going to catch you
and make you SORRY!"

31

But Little Crab had backed under a rock
and Jaguar could not catch him.

If you go to the beach
You will find Little Crab *still hiding* under his rock.
For Jaguar never did catch him.

NOTES ON TELLING

I heard Augusta Baker tell this tale at the Washoe County Public Library in Reno, Nevada, in the spring of 1970. As I drove back over the Sierras to Sacramento, I repeated her story over and over. The next day I began telling it, and this tale has been part of my working repertoire ever since. I was unable to find a printed source for the tale until recently.

If you would like to use audience participation with this story, pause before Little Crab begins to perform for Jaguar and ask the audience to help you say Little Crab's magic-eye sailing chant. You will have to go slowly and gather the audience with you as you chant. I told this story for years without audience participation, but added the participation technique recently as a vehicle for binding pre-school listeners to the tale. The story never fails to delight young children, and its imagery seems to stay with them.

A crab's eyes actually do stick out of its head on tiny stalks. You might want to mention this or show a picture of a crab either before or after the story. Children may not know what a jaguar is. You can define it briefly with a line within the story, or mention it before you begin the tale.

COMPARATIVE NOTES

The only printed English-language source I have found for this tale is Valery Carrick's "The Crab and the Jaguar" in *Picture Folk-Tales*. Carrick gives no source for the tale. There is, however, a German-language version of the tale in *Indianermärchen aus Südamerica* by Theodor Koch-Grünberg (p. 131-133). Koch-Grünberg ascribes the tale to the Taulipang Indians and places this group near the border of Brazil and British Guyana. Koch-Grünberg's tales are mostly translations of material written down by British and Dutch missionaries and ethnographers. It is amazing to see in South America this well-developed variant of a tale that is usually associated with North American Indian cultures.

Since my version was reconstructed from memory after hearing one telling by Augusta Baker, it differs from the printed sources. Koch-Grünberg calls the swallowing fish an "Animale-Podale." Carrick's vulture *makes* new eyes for jaguar rather than fetching berries.

The removable-eyes motif is a common one in Native American tales, especially in the western part of the United States. It is described as Motif J2423 *The eye-juggler. A trickster sees a man throwing his eyes into the air and replacing them. He also receives this power but he must not use the power beyond a specified number of times. When he does so, he loses his eyes. He usually gets animal eyes as substitutes.* Stith Thompson's *Tales of the North American Indians* (p. 299) lists variants from 29 Native American groups, a Siberian variant, and the above mentioned South American Indian variant.

This tale is often told of Coyote. In Eleanor Heady's *Sage Smoke: Tales of the Shoshoni-Bannock Indians* (p. 42-45) Ejapa, Coyote, sees two girls throwing their eyes into the air. The eyes become blue camas flowers when they fall. Coyote tries this without learning the magic words, and his eyes stick in a willow tree, which then becomes a pussy willow. Coyote, unable to see, stumbles over a dead buffalo calf and takes its eyes, which accounts for the fact that coyotes have such large eyes (MacDonald A2332.3.1.1).

Corinne Running's *When Coyote Walked the Earth: Indian Tales of the Pacific Northwest* shows Grouse tossing his eyes into the air. Coyote persuades him to trade eyes, but when Coyote tries the game Buzzard snatches his eyes. Coyote uses flowers for eyes, then trades flower eyes for Bird Boy (Snowbird)'s eyes.

In *Coyote Stories of the Navajo People* by Robert A. Roessel, Jr. and Dillon Platero (p. 99-102), Coyote sees small birds throwing their eyes into the air as they slide down a hillside on a rock. He begs them to teach him how to play and on his fourth try his eyes do not come back. The birds make eyes of pine pitch for him, but these melt when he gets near a fire, and this is why coyotes have yellow eyes.

In an Eskimo tale by Charles Gilham from *Beyond the Clapping Mountains* (p. 76-85), Crane substitutes blueberries for eyes after he has left them on a tree and Kayak has stolen them (MacDonald A2332.5.11). The berry motif in my version of "Little Crab and the Magic Eyes" is taken from this tale.

Several African tales explain why Crab's eyes lift out of his body, but lack the eye-juggling motif. See MacDonald and Thompson A2231.10 *Crab beats deity's forbidden drum: eyes lift out of body* (Fjort variant) and MacDonald A2320.41* *Crab tricks elephant and hawk. They behead him and throw into pond. Prawn puts eyes on shoulders* (Ikom, Eastern Nigerian variant). See also MacDonald and Thompson A2231.1.3 *Discourteous answer: why crab has eyes behind* (Polish, Estonian, and Lithuanian variants).

GROUNDHOG DANCE

Once seven wolves caught a groundhog.

They said:
"Now we will *kill* you
and EAT YOU UP."

The groundhog said:
"You will *eat* me.
I cannot help *that*.

But when you have good food
you should rejoice and give thanks
as the Indian does in his Green Corn Dance.

I have a good song and dance
that I could teach you."

The wolves always like to learn a new song and dance.

So they said:
> "All right.
> You teach us your song and dance.
> and *then*
> We'll EAT YOU UP."

Groundhog said:
> "I will go to each of seven trees
> and I will sing seven songs.
> When I sing my songs
> you wolves all dance away from me
> *in a straight line.*
>
> When I call 'YUH!'
> You wolves all turn
> and dance back toward me
> *in a straight line.*
>
> When I have sung my seventh and last song
> you may turn and chase me.
> The wolf that catches me...
> He may EAT ME UP."

The wolves lined up
  in a very straight line.

Groundhog went to the first tree
  and leaned against it.
He began to sing his first song.
He sang:

"HO wi YE a HI...
HO wi YE a HI..."

And the wolves danced away from him
in a *straight line*.

"Very Good!"
said Groundhog.
"Very good dancing."

Groundhog went to the second tree.
He sang his second song.
He sang:
"HI ya YU u WE...
HI ya YU u WE..."

And the wolves all danced away from him
in a *straight line*.

Groundhog called "YUH!"

And the wolves danced back toward him
in a *straight line*.

"Very Good!"
said Groundhog.
"Good dancing!"

Groundhog went to each of seven trees.
Groundhog sang seven songs.

The wolves did not know
each tree was a little closer
to Groundhog's hole under an old stump.

When Groundhog came to the last tree
    he said:
        "Now I will sing my seventh and *last* song.
        When I have finished
        all of you wolves may turn and *chase* me.
        The wolf that catches me...
        HE may EAT ME UP."

    "All right,"
    said the wolves.
    "All right."

The wolves lined up in a very straight line.
Groundhog sang until the wolves were dancing
    far away...in a *straight line*.
Groundhog sang:
        "HA...ya...HA...Ha...HA...
        HA...ya...HA...Ha...HA..."

Then when the wolves were dancing far away...
    in a straight line.
Groundhog called YUH!
and ran for his hole under the old stump.

All of the wolves turned and chased him
and the first wolf caught him by the end
    of his tail

just as he popped into his hole.

But the Groundhog's tail broke off.

And the Groundhog got away.

Still
From that day to this
groundhogs have very short tails.

And all groundhogs sing very sweet songs.
If you could only
hear them.

NOTES ON TELLING

This short story with its pattern of repetition is easy
to learn. The folklore collection from which I learned the tale
does not give notation for the groundhog's song, so I have
included the tune I made up. You may prefer to make up
your own tune. This tale, in your telling, will be far removed
from the authentic Cherokee tale. I have even changed the
syllables of Groundhog's song in my own tellings in order
to add a joke in his final song "Ha ya Ha Ha Ha." I also added
the final line about groundhogs singing very sweet songs.

As a folklorist, I would strongly criticize this kind of
tampering. As a storyteller, I make the tale my own and play
with it. I change the tale to delight my audience and myself.
I do not tell audiences that I am presenting an authentic
Cherokee legend when I tell this tale. If I am telling to adults
or older children, I may mention the ways in which I have
altered the tale.

Here is the tune I use. Katharine Judson, in *Myths*

and Legends of the Mississippi Valley and the Great Lakes gives Groundhog's song first as "Ho wi ye a hi," then as "Hi ya yu we." No music is given. See the comparative notes here for James Mooney's variant of the song text.

Slowly, resonantly, with firm beat

Ho   wi   ye   a   Hi_____

I do not usually use audience participation with this tale. However, it can easily be adapted by encouraging the children to join Groundhog in his chants. You may want to repeat the chants more than once to allow the children a chance to pick up the refrain and join in with you on the second chorus.

This tale can be stretched or shortened depending on how many of Groundhog's seven songs you sing. The tale lends itself to creative dramatic play, and I have found that pre-school as well as primary children respond to the story and enjoy acting it out.

COMPARATIVE NOTES

My version of this tale is based on Katharine B. Judson's variant in *Myths and Legends of the Mississippi Valley and the Great Lakes* (p. 169-170). Burdette S. Fitzgerald includes this variant in *World Tales for Creative Dramatics and Storytelling* (p. 287).

James Mooney published the tale in his "Myths of the Cherokee" in the *Nineteenth Annual Report of the Bureau of American Ethnology...1897-98* (p. 279). He says of the tale:

> This story is from Swimmer, the supplementary part being added by John Ax. The Groundhog dance is one of those belonging to the great thanksgiving ceremony, Green-corn dance. It consists of alternate advances

and retreats by the whole line of dancers in obedience to signals by the song leader, who sings to the accompaniment of a rattle. The burden of the song, which is without meaning is

Ha'wiye'ĕhi' Yaha'wiye'ĕhi (twice) Yu-u
Hi'yagu'wĕ Hahi'yagu'wĕ (twice) Yu-yu...(p. 452).

The tale is given in Coryden Bell's *John Rattling Gourd of Big Cove: A Collection of Cherokee Indian Legends* (p. 83-86). Bell cites as sources both Mooney and Mary E. Ulmer, Librarian at Qualla School, who heard these tales from her Cherokee friends and shared them with the author. The Qualla Indian Reservation is at Cherokee, North Carolina.

This tale also appears in Natalia Belting, *The Long-Tailed Bear and Other Indian Legends* (p. 29-33) and in George P. Scheer, *Cherokee Animal Tales* (p. 31-32). Scheer uses Mooney's exact text whenever possible. Eileen Colwell's *The Magic Umbrella and Other Stories for Telling* (p. 70) and Ruth Manning-Sanders' *Tortoise Tales* (p. 36-46) both include a Native American variant of the tale with a hare as protagonist. The wolves' dance is similar, but the text of the chant is different.

This tale is indexed under Thompson Motif K606 *Escape by singing song. Captive gradually moves away and at last escapes* and K606.2 *Escape by persuading captors to dance.* The notion of tricking a captor to sing or dance while one escapes is widespread. Thompson lists variants from Africa: Kaffir, Basuto, Gold Coast, Wachaga; India; Indonesia; and a related motif from Iceland and Ireland in which watchmen are sung to sleep. Kenneth Clarke's *Motif-Index of the Folk Tales of Culture Area V West Africa* lists three West African variants.

MacDonald lists an Eskimo variant of K606 in which mouse tricks fox (Charles Gilham, *Beyond the Clapping Mountains: Eskimo Stories from Alaska*, p. 99-105), a Kazakh variant in which sheep dance and escape (Mary Lou Masey, *Stories of the Steppes: Kazakh Folktales*, p. 116-117) and an Indian variant in which the leader of ten cloth merchants sings in code, instructing them to attack the three robbers (Joseph Jacobs, *Indian Folk and Fairy Tales*, p. 160-163).

Under K606.2 *Escape by persuading captors to dance* MacDonald lists an Eskimo variant in which weasel tricks raven (Ronald Melzack, *The Day Tuk Became a Hunter and Other Eskimo Stories*, p. 71-78), a Bering Strait Eskimo variant in which raven tricks marmot (Jean Cothran, *The Magic Calabash: Folk Tales from America's Lands and Alaska*, p. 22-24), a Byelorussian variant in which geese trick wolf (Mirra Ginsburg, *The Lazies: Tales of the People of Russia*, p. 12-17), and a Makah tale in which Kwatee persuades wolves to dance (Emerson Matson, *Legends of the Great Chiefs*, p. 103-106).

The tale's ending uses Thompson Motif A2378.4 *Why animal has short tail*. This is a favorite motif in children's folktale collections. MacDonald cites 27 sources giving explanations for the short tails of hare, bear, crow, wren, deer, lynx, coyote, wolf, bobcat, wildcat, elephant, and groundhog.

OLD ONE-EYE

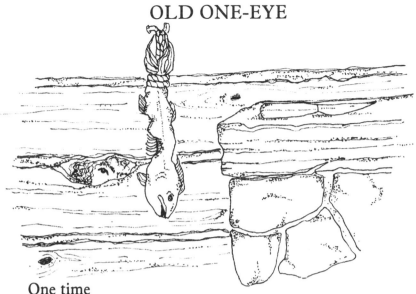

One time
there was an old woman
lived way up in the hills
in a log cabin all by herself.

Now she'd been savin' her money
and savin' her money
till she was just about *rich*.

She kept her money in a leather pouch
hid way up in the chimney corner.

Every night that old lady would sit there
and she would rock
      back and forth...
      back and forth...
and she would card her wool.
      ...scritch..scratch...
      ...scritch..scratch...
      ...scritch..scratch...

Rockin'...and a-cardin'...
   ...scritch..scratch...
   ...scritch..scratch...
   ...scritch..scratch...

After she'd been sittin' there for awhile
she'd commence to *yawn.*

   "Awwwwwwwwnnnnn"

And after she'd yawned *three times...*
She figured it was time to go to bed.

Now over on the wall by the chimney
she had hangin' a big dried *fish.*

Just hangin' there by its tail
with its eye *starin'* out into the room...

That fish had only one eye
so she called it *"Old One-Eye."*

Before she'd go to bed
she'd go over and she'd get out her butcher knife...
and she'd cut a chunk off of Old One-Eye.

And she'd *chew* it up and go to bed.

Well, they was THREE ROBBERS come into the area.
And they heard about her gold.

44

So they went up there one night
  a-fixin' to *rob* her.

The chief of the robbers...
he had only one eye in his head
on account of he'd got the other one
  put out in a fight.
And because of that he was known as
  "Old One-Eye."

This Old One-Eye took his men up into the holler
behind that old woman's house
and he hid them there.

    "We'll wait
    till she goes to bed.
    Then we'll go up there and
    steal her gold."

He called the first robber:
    "YOU! You go up there
    and spy on that old woman
    and when she goes to bed
    you come back here and tell us.
    We'll go up there
    and ROB HER!"

So the first robber went up to the cabin.
He found a chink between the logs
right up alongside the chimney
where he could look in.

He put his eyes up to that chink
and *looked* into the cabin.

She was a-sittin' there.
A-rockin'…and a-cardin'…
A-rockin'…and a-cardin'…
        Scritch..scratch…
        scritch..scratch…
        scritch..scratch…

Pretty soon

        "Awwwwnnnn" (she yawned)

        "Well that's *one*
        that's come.
        Two more come
        and I'll get my butcher knife."

And she looked over at that old *one-eyed fish*
    hangin' on the wall by the chimney.

To that robber
    it appeared that she was lookin'
    right at him.

LAWS!
He jumped up and ran back down that holler.

        "That lady's a WITCH!
        She looked right through that wall and SAW me!

46

OLD ONE-EYE

Said 'That's *one* that's come
and if *two more* come
I'm gettin' my BUTCHER KNIFE!'
Let's *get out of here* men!"

"Such NONSENSE"
said old One-Eye the robber chief.
"That old woman couldn't have seen you.
You were just scared."

"YOU!" He called the second robber.
"YOU go up there
and spy on that old woman.
Soon as she goes to bed
You come back down here and tell us.
And we'll go up and
STEAL HER GOLD."

So the second robber went up to the cabin.
He put his eyes up to the chink between the logs...
and he could see her in there all right...

A-rocking and a-cardin'...
and a-rockin' and a-cardin'...
    Scritch..scratch...
    scritch..scratch...
    scritch..scratch...

First thing you know...

    "Awwwwwnnnnn

47

Now that's *two* that's come.
One more comes
it'll be time to get out my butcher knife."

The second robber JUMPED up.
ran out of there back down to the hollow.

"JIMINY! That old lady *is* a witch!
She said 'That's *two* that's come
and if *one more* comes
I'm gettin' out my butcher knife.'
We'd better get out of *here*."

"Well you fellows are just plain *chicken*."
said Old One-Eye.
"I'm gonna have to go up there *myself*
and see what's goin' on."

So Old One-Eye himself...
HE went up there
and he put his one good eye up to that chink between
the logs
and he *looked* into that cabin...

And she was still a-sittin' there all right.
She hadn't gone to bed yet.
Sittin' there a-rockin...and a-cardin'...
and a-rockin'...and a-cardin'...

Then

48

OLD ONE-EYE

"Awwwnnnnn!
GOODNESS GRACIOUS ME!
That's *three* that's come.
Time to get out my butcher knife
and cut a chunk out of *you...*
OLD ONE-EYE!!"

And she come for that one-eyed fish.
Laws that robber jumped up
and run back down that holler

    "She's a WITCH she's a WITCH ALL RIGHT!
    She come for me with a BUTCHER KNIFE
      and called me by NAME!
    LET'S GET OUT OF HERE men!"

And they tore out of there
and never come back no more.

That old woman
just *got out her butcher knife*
and went along over and cut a big chunk
   out of the old one-eyed fish
and *chawed* it up real good
and went to bed and slept *right sound*.

NOTES ON TELLING

A marvelous rendition of this tale by Virginia Hendricks can be seen in the film "There's Something About a Story." That telling seemed so perfect that I didn't even attempt to tell the tale for years. This year I finally felt ready to tell "Old One-Eye," perhaps because I am now old enough to identify with the old woman.

My telling uses audience response. I mime the rocking motion "Back...and forth..." and the carding motion "scritch...scratch...." The children soon join in the motions. Many even "YAWNNNN" with me, though I don't attempt to elicit that response.

I tell this tale in a fairly heavy dialect using my own southern Indiana speech patterns. If the dialect doesn't feel right for you, reset it in your own idiom.

COMPARATIVE NOTES

This telling is taken from Richard Chase's *Grandfather Tales* (p. 205-212). Chase got the tale from Ben Hall in Hayesville, North Carolina. Burton Lowrimore collected a version of this tale from his mother, who had heard it in Fort Smith, Arkansas, around 1890 from her father, who heard it as a Confederate soldier in the Civil War. ("Six California Tales" in *California Folklore Quarterly*, V. 4, 1945, p. 154-156). Lowrimore points out that the first written form of this tale may have been in Heinrich Bebel's Latin jests of 1508. In Lowrimore's version an old woman catches a one-eyed fish, hangs it up by the chimney, sits down to spin, counts her hiccups, and then eats supper. "Come down old one eye and I'll have you for supper." Three men are hiding on the roof, two run away, but the third, who has only one eye, is so scared that he falls down the chimney.

This American tale seems unique in its use of the one-eyed fish motif. European variants of the tale are often called "The Three Yawns." German, Danish, French, and Italian variants of this tale are listed in J. Bolte and G. Polívka, *Anmerkungen zu den Kinder- und Hausmärchen*, II (p. 412).

Children's librarians will recognize the tale's similarity to the Grimms' "Dr. Know-it-all" (Doctor Allwissend). In variants of this tale a sham wise man counts to himself and hiding thieves think themselves detected and confess. Type 1641 *Doctor Know-All* lists numerous variants: German, Finnish, Swedish, Estonian, Livonian, Lithuanian, Lappish, Norwegian, Icelandic, Irish, French, Spanish, Dutch, Flemish, Walloon, Italian, Sicilian, Hungarian, Czechoslovakian, Slovenian, Serbocroatian, Russian, Greek, Turkish, Indian, Indonesian, Chinese, English-American, Spanish-American (Argentina, Dominican Republic, Puerto Rico, West Indies), and American Black (Michigan, Georgia).

MacDonald lists several children's versions as N611.1 *Criminal accidentally detected: "that is the first"—sham wise man.* These include an unusual Burmese variant in which an opium eater talking to his supper frightens off robbers with names such as "Lobster" (Eleanor Brockett, *Burmese and Thai Fairy Tales*, p. 63-66). A Korean variant shows an old man telling a story to himself as he watches a crane moving about the field: "He comes...he creeps..." and the robber flees (Paul Anderson, *The Boy and the Blind Storyteller*, p. 53-58, and Frances Carpenter, *Tales of a Korean Grandmother*, p. 183-188).

Additional discussion of this tale may be found in Clarkson and Cross, *World Folktales* (p. 73-74).

PARLEY GARFIELD AND THE FROGS

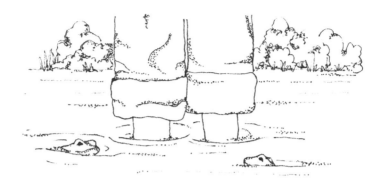

Now when my grandpa, Parley Garfield, was a boy
He had to cross the crick to see my grandma
   every night.

Most times in the summer
when the cricks run dry
he could just *walk* across
on the flat rocks.

But in the spring
when the hard rains came
that crick would flood.

Then he'd come down to the edge of the crick
and he wouldn't know whether or not
   it was too deep to wade through.

Now there was a family of frogs
that lived at the place
   where the crick pooled there.
And they'd come along and help him out.

PARLEY GARFIELD AND THE FROGS

Grandpa'd call out to the frogs:
  "How DEEP is it?
  How DEEP is it?
  How DEEP is it?"

Now the little ones at the edge of the crick
they'd call back:
     "Ankledeep!
     Ankledeep!
     Ankledeep!"

So Grandpa'd take off his shoes and wade in a bit.
Out a little further the frogs grew a little bigger.
Grandpa'd call to them:
  "How DEEP is it?
  How DEEP is it?
  How DEEP is it?"

And that bunch of frogs would call right back:
     "Kneedeep!
     Kneedeep!
     Kneedeep!"

So Grandpa, he'd roll up his pants legs and wade in a
  little more.

Then he'd call to the big old frogs
  way out toward the middle.

     "How DEEP is it?
     How DEEP is it?
     How DEEP is it?"

They'd holler back:
"Bellydeep!
Bellydeep!
Bellydeep!"

Grandpa wanted to see grandma awfully bad.
So he'd just wade right on in up to his belly
    and get all wet.
Then he'd stop.
And Grandpa'd call out to that old Grandaddy Bullfrog
        Lived right out in the middle of the pond:

        "How DEEP is it?
        How DEEP is it?
        How DEEP is it?

And that old Grandaddy Bullfrog'd bellow back:
"YOU BETTER GO ROUND!
YOU BETTER GO ROUND!
YOU BETTER GO ROUND!"

Then Grandpa knew he'd have to go round and find
another place to ford the crick *that* night
if he wanted to see Grandma at all.

I've heard my grandpa
tell that story
many a time.

NOTES ON TELLING

When telling to pre-schoolers and early primary children, I encourage them to join me on the frogs' calls throughout the telling. I make Grandpa's call to the frogs repetitive by using the chant "How DEEP is it?" every time, and let the children join in on that chant also.

After the brief tale telling, let the group make the frogs' calls with you. With older groups you can divide into four parts and form a frogs' chorus. Cue each group in one at a time starting with the "Ankledeepers."

With a little practice you can make the frog's calls sound much like real frogs calling. The "Ankledeep!" should be high and sharp. Hold the "Aaannn..." sound making it slightly nasal, then flip off into a quick "kledeep!" Lower your voice for each water level. "Bellydeep" should be resonant. "You better go ROUND" should ring! I've included musical notation you might find helpful.

How deep is it?

An-kle deep! An-kle deep! An-kle deep! An-kle deep!

Knee deep! Knee deep! Knee deep! Knee deep!

Bel-ly deep! Bel-ly deep! Bel-ly deep! Bel-ly deep!

You bet-ter go 'round!   You bet-ter go 'round!

COMPARATIVE NOTES

Each family has its own stock of tales. This one has been a long time favorite in my family, but it is often hard to identify the tales in one's own family lore. It wasn't until I heard the tale related by Joseph Du Puis, a Potowatami and Sac/Fox Indian now living in Washington state, that I realized this was a story. Mr. Du Puis told the tale as he had heard it from *his* grandfather.

Though I have located no print sources for this tale, the story seems widely known. Sally Porter-Smith, of Centralia, Washington, reports hearing the story from her Canadian grandmother. If this is one of your family stories too, just substitute your grandfather's name for Parley Garfield.

THE
LITTLE ROOSTER
AND THE TURKISH SULTAN

Some where...
some place...
across the Seven Seas...
There lived a Little Old Lady
and her Little Pet Rooster.

One day
the Little Rooster went out into the yard
to peck out something to eat.
He pecked and he pecked and he pecked
and he pecked out
a *diamond button!*

> "COCK-A-DOODLE-DOOOO!"
>   said the Little Rooster.
> "I *like* diamond buttons!
> I'll take this home to my good mistress.
> *She* likes diamond buttons *too!*"

He picked the diamond button up in his beak
and started to walk home.

Just then along came the Turkish Sultan.
He was the man who ruled the land of Turkey.
He was a *very large* Turkish Sultan.
He wore a pair of big baggy trousers.
His pants were *so* baggy
that he had to have three servants walk behind him
to hold his trousers up.

He came *walking* down the road...
And his three servants came behind
holding up his trousers.

When he saw the Little Rooster with the
    diamond button...
He wanted that diamond button for himself.

THE LITTLE ROOSTER

He called his three servants and said:
    "You CATCH that Little Rooster.
    Take his diamond button from him.
    And put it in MY treasure chamber in the palace."

The three servants *caught* the Little Rooster.
They *took* his diamond button.
And put it in the Turkish Sultan's *treasure chamber*.

The Little Rooster was *so* angry,

He flew right to the Turkish Sultan's palace.
He perched up on the window sill
and he called out:
    "COCK-A-DOODLE-DOOOO!
    Turkish Sultan!
    You GIVE ME BACK MY DIAMOND
        BUTTON!"

The Turkish Sultan was *mad* when he heard that.
He called his three servants and said:
    "You CATCH that Little Rooster.
    Throw him into a WELL FULL OF WATER.
    And that will be the end of HIM."

The three servants caught the Little Rooster
and threw him into a *well full of water*.

But the Little Rooster
had a
magic stomach.

As soon as he was in the well he called out:
    "Come my Empty Stomach...
    Come my Empty Stomach...
    Drink up ALL the water in this well."

His stomach began to drink.
He *drank* and *drank* and *drank*...
He drank up *all* the water in that well.

He got *very* big
But he didn't drown!

Instead
He flew right back to the Turkish Sultan's palace.
He perched on the window sill.
And he called out:
    "COCK-A-DOODLE-DOOOOO!
    Turkish Sultan!
    You GIVE ME BACK MY DIAMOND
        BUTTON!"

The Turkish Sultan was *angry* when he heard that.
He called his three servants and said:
    "You catch that Little Rooster
    and throw him into a FIRE.
    That will be the end of HIM."

The three servants *caught* the Little Rooster
and threw him into a *fire*.
But the Little Rooster called out:

60

THE LITTLE ROOSTER

"Come my FULL STOMACH...
Come my FULL STOMACH...
Spit out all the water from the well
and PUT OUT THE FIRE."

The Little Rooster's stomach
spit out *all* the water from the well
and put out the fire.
So it couldn't burn him at all.

Instead
He flew right back to the Turkish Sultan's palace.
He perched on the window sill
and he called out:
    "COCK-A-DOODLE-DOOOOO!
    Turkish Sultan!
    You GIVE ME BACK MY DIAMOND
        BUTTON!"

The Turkish Sultan was *furious.*

He called his three servants and said:
    "Catch that Little Rooster
    and throw him into a BEE HIVE.
    Let the bees just STING him."

The three servants caught the Little Rooster
and threw him into a *bee hive.*

But the Little Rooster called out:
    "Come my EMPTY STOMACH...

Come my EMPTY STOMACH...
Eat up ALL THE BEES IN THE BEE HIVE!"

His stomach ate up
All the bees in the bee hive.

They buzzed around inside
But they couldn't sting his magic stomach.

Instead
The Little Rooster flew right back to the
   Turkish Sultan's palace.

He perched on the window sill
And he called out:
   "COCK-A-DOODLE-DOOOOO!
   Turkish Sultan!
   You GIVE ME BACK MY DIAMOND
     BUTTON!"

The Turkish Sultan was *infuriated.*

He called his three servants and said:
   "You catch that Little Rooster
     and bring him to ME.
   What will I DO with him?"

The first servant said:
   "If *I* were you I would CHOP his head off."

The second servant said:

62

THE LITTLE ROOSTER

"If *I* were you I would HANG HIM
from the highest tree."

But the *third* servant said:
"If *I* were you, I know what *I* would do with him!
I would SIT ON HIM AND SQUASH HIM!"

This was a very good idea
because the Turkish Sultan was a *very heavy*
Turkish Sultan.

He said:
"CATCH that Little Rooster.
DROP him into the big bag
on my baggy pants behind
and...*let*...*me*...SIT...*on him*
and SQUASH *him*!"

So they caught the Little Rooster
and dropped him into the big bag
on the Turkish Sultan's baggy pants.

But the Little Rooster called out:
"Come my FULL STOMACH
Come my FULL STOMACH
Let out all the BEES!
and STING that Turkish Sultan!"

The Little Rooster's stomach let out all the *bees*.

Did they *sting* that Turkish Sultan????!!!!

"Oh OH!!
OW OW!!
OOO OOO!!"

The Turkish Sultan was jumping around his throne room.

He cried:
"Catch that Little Rooster.
Take him to my treasure chamber
and let him HAVE his old diamond button.
I never want to SEE HIM again."

They took the Little Rooster
to the Turkish Sultan's treasure chamber.

They said:
"TAKE your diamond button
and GO ALONG HOME."

They left him *all alone*
in the Turkish Sultan's treasure chamber.
The Little Rooster *looked around*.
He saw all the *diamonds*
all the *gold and silver*
all the *emeralds and rubies*
in the Turkish Sultan's treasure chamber

So he called out:
"Come my EMPTY STOMACH
Come my EMPTY STOMACH
Eat up ALL the TREASURE
in the Turkish Sultan's treasure chamber."

64

THE LITTLE ROOSTER

His stomach
ate up all the gold and silver
all the emeralds and rubies
all the *diamonds*
in the Turkish Sultan's treasure chamber.

And when he was *very* full...
He waddled along home
and gave it all to his good mistress.

And they lived richly
and happily
ever after.

NOTES ON TELLING

I acquired this tale in a rather unusual way. I was examining new books in Seattle Public Library's children's department one day in 1964 when I realized that someone was telling stories just behind the partition where I was sitting. I began to listen and heard a delightful story about a little rooster and a Turkish sultan. The story was so memorable that I was able to begin telling it from that one hearing. Though I never learned the name of the teller, a bit of research unearthed a source for this tale in Kate Seredy's *The Good Master*. After twenty years of telling, my own version is still remarkably similar to Seredy's rendition.

This is my all-time favorite story for kindergarten telling. I encourage the children to chime in on Little Rooster's crows. We usually practice a few crows before I begin the story and we let our "COCK-a-doodle-DOOOOOOOS!" ring right to the rafters. We pound one fist into the other in anger as Little Rooster demands "Give me back my diamond button!" Younger groups especially enjoy this fist-pounding.

This tale works well with pre-school as well as primary children. Most children younger than kindergarten will not have figured out the bees in the pants bit until it actually happens. With older groups you can pause as Little Rooster calls to his empty stomach to let out all the...Let the children supply the gleefully horrid answer...BEES!!!

One second grade class at the Singapore American School absolutely refused to let me tell any other story in my weekly story session until I had repeated this tale first. The tale soon became group drama as everyone learned all the lines.

If you do not explain before you begin that there is a country called Turkey, younger children will think the Turkish Sultan is a "big turkey"; perhaps the *Turkey's* Sultan. I'm not sure this hurts the story from the point of view of the younger listener. Older children, however, might find it interesting to know something about the background of the story. The fact that a little Hungarian rooster should defeat a *Turkish* Sultan is historically meaningful.

Be sure to take plenty of time with the lovely, magical introduction to this story. And pause at the ending to let the children all join you in the fulfilling "happily...*ever after.*"

COMPARATIVE NOTES

Swallowing tales are popular in children's collections. This tale is related to Aarne-Thompson Type 2027 *The Fat Cat*. See comparative notes in this book on "Sody Sallyrytus" for discussion of another Type 2027 tale.

The MacDonald and Thompson Motif-Indexes classify Type 2027 as Z33.2 *The fat cat* and list variants in which cat, pig, troll, and louse are villains. In each case the greedy animal consumes everything and everyone in sight, growing fatter and fatter.

"The Little Rooster and the Turkish Sultan" and its variants differ from the "Fat Cat" tales in that the swallower is a hero, not a villain. This tale is Thompson Motif number Z52 *Bird avenges caged mate.* Thompson lists one Indian variant in which a bird collects cat, ants, rope, club, and river in his ear. He is put into the king's fowl house where the cat eats chickens, put in the king's bedroom where he releases the flood, etc. A children's picture book *Rum Pum Pum* by Maggie Duff uses this Indian tale.

A well known children's variant of Z52 is the French *Drakestail.* His chant "Quack Quack Quack. I want my MONEY back!" makes excellent storytime fare. MacDonald's *Storyteller's Sourcebook* lists eight sources for *Drakestail,* including Jan Wahl's excellent I-Can-Read picture book *Drakestail.* Other variants include a Joel Chandler Harris version in which Teenchy-tiny duck is the hero (*The Complete Tales of Uncle Remus,* p. 760-771); a Swiss variant with Red Chicken; a Brazilian version with Little White Hen; a Portuguese variant with a Tipsy Rooster; and the Spanish "Medio-Pollito."

In unusual Polish and Russian variants, an old woman or old man climbs a magic growing beanstalk or oak tree to the sky, bringing back a cock and other magic object. The magic object is stolen and the cock recovers it by swallowing fire, well water, and others. This is an interesting combination of a *Jack and the Beanstalk* motif with Z52.

The variant of *The Little Rooster and the Turkish Sultan* included in this book is modeled closely on Kate Seredy's retelling in her novel *The Good Master* (p. 122-127). MacDonald also lists picture book versions by Victor Ambrus (*The Little Cockerel*), and Jeanne Hardendorff (*The Little Cock*). See also Mirra Ginsburg, *The Magic Stove.*

For additional discussion of this tale, consult Clarkson and Cross, *World Folktales* (p. 225-228).

THE GUNNY WOLF

Once there was a little girl
who lived with her mother
at the edge of a *deep dark* forest.
The mother always told the little girl:
      "Whatever you do... *don't* go into the FOREST.
      Because the *Gunny Wolf* might get you!"

The little girl always promised
   that she would *never* go into the forest.

One day the mother had to go away to the village.
Before she left she warned the little girl:
      "Remember what I told you.
      Don't *even go near* the forest.
      Because if you *do*...
      the GUNNY WOLF might get you!"

68

THE GUNNY WOLF

The little girl promised
    that she would *never* go into the forest.
But as soon as her mother had gone
the little girl saw some little blue flowers
blooming right at the edge of the forest.

        "Oh I *must* pick those little blue flowers,"
            said the little girl.

And she went *just* to the edge of the forest
and began to pick the flowers.

And as she picked she *sang*:
        "Kum-kwa...Ki-wa...
        Kum-kwa...Ki-wa..."

Then the little girl saw...
deeper in the forest...
some *white* flowers.
They were so lacy and beautiful...
she just *had* to pick *them* too.

So the little girl went *deeper* into the forest
and began to pick the *white* flowers.

        "Kum-kwa...Ki-wa...
        Kum-kwa...Ki-wa..."

Just then
deep deep in the forest
she saw some bright RED flowers!
They were *so* beautiful that she just *had* to pick *them*.

69

So the little girl went *deep deep* into the forest
and began to pick the *red* flowers.

> "Kum-kwa...Ki-wa...
> Kum-kwa...Ki-wa...
> Kum-kwa...Ki-wa..."

When suddenly
UP sprang the GUNNY WOLF!!!

> "Little Girl!
> You sing that GUTEN SWEETEN SONG
> AGAIN!"
> said the Gunny Wolf in his big hoarse voice.

So the little girl had to sing her song.
> "Kum-kwa...Ki-wa...
> Kum-kwa...Ki-wa..."

And while she sang
the old Gunny Wolf fell fast asleep.

As soon as he was asleep
off tiptoed the little girl
Pit-a-pat...Pit-a-pat...Pit-a-pat....

But UP rose the GUNNY WOLF!
And *after* her he came.

70

HUNKER-CHA...HUNKER-CHA...
HUNKER-CHA...HUNKER-CHA...

And he *caught* her.

> "Little Girl
> Why FOR you MOVE?"

> "I no move."

> "Then sing that GUTEN SWEETEN song
> AGAIN."

So little girl had to sing.
> "Kum-kwa...Ki-wa...
> Kum-kwa...Ki-wa..."

And as she sang
the Gunny Wolf fell fast asleep.

Then off ran the little girl.
Pit-a-pat...pit-a-pat...pit-a-pat...pit-a-pat....

But UP sprang the GUNNY WOLF!

HUNKER-CHA...HUNKER-CHA...
HUNKER-CHA...HUNKER-CHA...

And he *caught* her.

> "Little girl why for you MOVE?"

"I no move."

"Then sing that GUTEN SWEETEN song
    AGAIN."

"Kum-kwa...Ki-wa...
Kum-kwa...Ki-wa...
Kum-kwa...Ki-wa..."

This time she sang a *long long* time
till the Gunny Wolf was *fast fast* asleep.

Then off ran the little girl.
Pit-a-pat...pit-a-pat...pit-a-pat...pit-a-pat...
...past the *red* flowers...
pit-a-pat...pit-a-pat...pit-a-pat...
...past the *white* flowers...
pit-a-pat...pit-a-pat...pit-a-pat...
...past the *blue* flowers...
pit-a-pat...pit-a-pat...pit-a-pat...
...out of the *forest*...
pit-a-pat...pit-a-pat...pit-a-pat...
...into her very own *house*...
...and SLAMMED THE DOOR!

And the little girl *never* went into the forest again.

THE GUNNY WOLF

NOTES ON TELLING

This is an excellent audience participation story for pre-school and primary grade children. I sometimes prepare the audience for the telling by asking them to roar like a Gunny Wolf "RRRARRR!!" It is hard to be afraid of a wolf when you are making his growls *for* him. Each time the mother mentions the horrid GUNNY WOLF, we give his frightening ROAR. And of course we all leap into action with outstretched claws and mighty roars with every "UP sprang the GUNNY WOLF!!"

The audience also joins in the little girl's gentle flower-picking song. I use a quiet, soothing, repetitive tune. Almost every teller has a different tune and pronunciation for this song. Feel free to make up your own. Here is my tune:

Kum-kwa   Ki - wa   Kum-kwa   Ki - wa

We all pat our knees lightly as the little girl "pit-a-pats" along. We "HUNKER-CHA!"...making exaggerated galloping motions with arms and rhythmic leg slapping as the Gunny Wolf chases after the little girl. When the Gunny Wolf falls fast asleep, we all lay our head to one side on our hands and snore lightly, and at the end we SLAM the door with a loud clap.

With primary school children I sometimes like to break the group into little girls and Gunny Wolves, letting each half chant the lines for their character as the story flows along. Mostly, though, everyone wants to do all the parts. If this story is told very many times, your audience will want to get on their feet and act it out.

COMPARATIVE NOTES

I learned "The Gunny Wolf" from Bob Polishuk,

73

storytelling instructor at the University of Washington in the summer of 1964. It is a popular tale and I have heard many tellers perform it. I am sure my version borrows a bit from each of them.

The best known printed version of this tale is that of Wilhelmina Harper. Her picture book rendition illustrated by William Wiesner (Dutton, 1967) is still in print and can be found on the shelves of most children's libraries.

A Maryland variant published in 1925 has the little girl living with her father. ("Folk-Lore from Maryland" by Annie Weston Whitney and Caroline Canfield Bullock, *Memoirs of the American Folk-Lore Society*, Vol XVII, 1925, p. 179). The dialogue runs:

"You move?" (Gruff voice)

"O no my dear, what 'casion I move?" (In childish voice)

"Sing that sweeten, gooden song again."

"Tray bla-tray bla-cum qua, kimo.

Pit-a-pat, pit-a-pat, pit-a-pat, pit-a-pat."

This tale is reminiscent of "Little Red Riding Hood" (K2011), but is more closely related in motif to K606 *Escape by singing song. Captive gradually moves away and at last escapes.* MacDonald lists an Eskimo variant of K606 in which mouse tricks fox, and another variant from the Russian steppes in which sheep escape from a wolf. (See tale notes in this book for "Groundhog Dance" for related variants.) Stith Thompson lists Kaffir and Cape Verde Island variants of this motif. Kenneth Clarke's West African motif-index lists one African variant. It would be interesting to know more about the origin of the American variant of this tale, which substitutes the encounter of a little girl and a wolf for the more usual encounter of a small and large animal.

HOW TO BREAK A BAD HABIT

Monkey and Rabbit sat talking.
Rabbit twitched his nose.
Monkey scratched his back.
Rabbit twitched his ear.
Monkey scratched his leg.
Rabbit twitched his other ear.
Monkey scratched his head.

"Would you STOP that TWITCHING," said
    Monkey.
"What a bad HABIT that is."

"Bad HABIT?" said Rabbit.
"Talk about bad HABITS...
Look at YOU.
Scratch...scratch...scratch...
Now that *is* a bad habit."

"Well *I* could easily STOP if I wanted to,"
said Monkey.
"So could *I* !" said Rabbit.

"We'll SEE!" said Monkey.

"Let's have a contest.
The first person to scratch or twitch LOSES.
Begin...when...I...say...GO!"

   "ALL RIGHT!"
Rabbit sat very still.
Monkey sat very still.

No one could scratch.
No one could twitch.

It was *very* hard to sit so still.

"Let's tell stories," said Rabbit.
"I'll tell you what happened yesterday."

And Rabbit began to talk.

"Yesterday I walked by the marsh.
And mosquitoes came after me.
One bit me *here*." (Rabbit twitched his nose
   to show where he was bitten.)
"One bit me *here*." (Rabbit twitched his ear.)

76

"Another bit me *here*." (Rabbit twitched his
   other ear.)
"And here...and here...and here..."
   (Rabbit was twitching like crazy.)

"Wait! Wait! *I'll* tell a story!" called Monkey.
"Yesterday *I* was walking in town.
And a little boy threw rocks at me.
He hit me *here*." (Monkey scratched his back.)
"He hit me *here*." (Monkey scratched his leg.)
"He hit me *here*." (Monkey scratched his head.)
"And here...and here...and here..."
   (Monkey was scratching all over.)

"I give up!" said Rabbit.

"Me too!" said Monkey.

Rabbit and Monkey began to laugh.
They laughed and laughed.

"After all," they said
"It's very HARD to BREAK A BAD HABIT."

NOTES ON TELLING

With pre-school children I preface this story with a
remark about the twitching and scratching habits of rabbits
and monkeys. We practice scratching like monkeys and

twitching like rabbits. They may join in with Monkey and Rabbit as they scratch and twitch in the story. Primary children delight in telling about their own bad habits. Afterward we may all sit very still and see how long we can refrain from itching or scratching. It's really hard not to scratch when you know you can't!

COMPARATIVE NOTES

This story appears in Frances Carpenter's *African Wonder Tales* (p. 41-45). A delightful variant is also found in Joel Chandler Harris' *Nights with Uncle Remus* (p. 214-222).

This tale is Motif K263 *Agreement not to scratch. In talking the trickster makes gestures and scratches without detection.* Thompson lists variants from India and Jamaica in addition to American Black variants from the southern United States. Kenneth Clarke's West African Motif-Index lists one variant.

MacDonald's *Storyteller's Sourcebook* lists related tales in which a story is told in order to give an excuse for making a certain gesture. From Portugal comes the tale of a friar who loosens his belt after a hefty meal by taking it off to show how long a serpent is. (Patricia Tracey Lowe, *The Little Horse of Seven Colors,* p. 30.) In a Nigerian suitor tale, the young man must stay in a room full of mosquitoes without driving them off. He tells a story that enables him to slap his body. When told to eat red peppers without grimacing, he shoos the chickens "Zoo...Zoo" (Barbara K. Walker, *Nigerian Folk Tales,* p. 57-58).

Thompson lists a related Motif K95 *Finger-drying contest won by deception. Three daughters are to wet hands: the first to have hands dry is to be the first to marry. The youngest waves her hands, exclaiming, "I don't want a man!"* She wins. Italian Novella and North Carolina variants are given.

SODY SALLYRYTUS

One time
There was an old man,
an old woman,
a little boy,
a little girl,
and a *pet squirrel* up on the mantlepiece.

The Old Woman went to the cupboard to make some
biscuits . . .
and she didn't have any *sody sallyrytus.*
That's *baking soda* you know.
To make the biscuits *rise.*

She called the Little Boy.
Says:

> "Little Boy.
> You go down to the *store*
> and buy me some *sody sallyrytus.*"

Little Boy went out.

He went *walking* down the road . . .
and *walking* down the road . . .
walking across the bridge . . .
went on down to the store and bought some
       Sody Sallyrytus.

Come *walking* back up the road . . .
Started *walking* across that *bridge* . . .

And an *old bear* stuck his head out from under that
BRIDGE!

      "WHO'S THAT WALKIN' OVER MY
      BRIDGE??!"

    "Just ME. Little Boy.
    Me and my Sody Sallyrytus."

    "Well I'm going to eat you UP!
    You and your Sody Sallyrytus TOO!"

And the Old Bear *swallowed* that Little Boy down.
Glump . . . Glump . . .
Just like *that.*

Little Boy didn't come home.
So the Old Woman called Little Girl.

  "Little Girl,
      run down to the store
      and see what's keeping Little Boy.
      He should've been *home* before now."

80

SODY SALLYRYTUS

Little Girl started out.
She went *walking* down the road . . .
and *walking* down the road . . .
started *walking* across that bridge . . .

AND THE OLD BEAR STUCK HIS HEAD OUT
FROM UNDER THAT BRIDGE!

"WHO'S THAT WALKIN' ACROSS MY
BRIDGE???!"

"Just ME.
Little Girl."

"Well, I ate the Little BOY. . .
Him and his *Sody Sallyrytus* TOO!
And I reckon I'll eat YOU up!"

And the Old Bear *swallowed* the Little Girl down.
Glump . . . Glump . . .
Just like *that.*

The Old Woman *waited* and she *waited* . . .
but the Little Girl didn't come *home.*

So the Old Woman called the Old Man.

"Old Man . . .
Go down to the store
and see why Little Boy and Little Girl
don't come home."

So Old Man went out.
He went *walking* down the road . . .
and *walking* down the road . . .
started *walking* across that bridge . . .

AND THAT OLD BEAR STUCK HIS HEAD OUT.

"WHO'S THAT WALKIN' ACROSS MY
    BRIDGE??!"
says the Old Bear.

"Just ME
Old Man."

"Well I ate the Little Girl.
And I ate the Little Boy.
Him and his *SODY SALLYRYTUS* TOO!

And I reckon I'm going to eat YOU!"

And that Old Bear *swallowed* the Old Man down.
Glump . . . Glump . . .
Just like *that*.

The Old Man didn't come home.
The Old Woman *waited* and she *waited* . . .
and finally she said:
    "I'm going to see what's *keeping* them."

And SHE went *walking* down the road . . .
and *walking* down the road . . .
and started *walking* across that bridge . . .

SODY SALLYRYTUS

AND THE OLD BEAR STUCK HIS HEAD OUT
FROM UNDER THAT BRIDGE.

"WHO'S THAT WALKIN' OVER MY
    BRIDGE??!"

"Just ME.
Old Woman."

"Well I ate the Old MAN.
And I ate the Little GIRL.
And I ate the Little BOY.
Him and his SODY SALLYRYTUS TOO.
And I reckon I'll eat YOU!"

And he *swallowed* her down.
Glump . . . glump . . .
Just like *that*.

Well who was *left*?

The pet squirrel
back home on the *mantlepiece*.

He went *running* up and down the mantlepiece . . .
and *running* up and down the mantlepiece . . .
Said:

"I'd better go see what's *keeping* those fool folks.
They should've come home and baked my *biscuits*
    before *now*."

And that squirrel went *skipping* out the door . . .
skipping down the road . . .
skipping down the road . . .
started *skipping* across that bridge . . .

And the OLD BEAR stuck his head out from under
that bridge!

"WHO'S THAT SKIPPING OVER MY
BRIDGE??!"

"Just ME.
Little Squirrel."

"Well I ate the Old Woman.
I ate the Old Man.
I ate the Little Girl.
And I ate the Little Boy.
Him and his SODY SALLYRYTUS TOO!
And I reckon I'm going to eat YOU up!"

And he *snapped* at that Little Squirrel . . .
But the Little Squirrel *ran* off of that bridge
and ran up the nearest *tree*!

The Old Bear was *mad.*

He came *climbing* out from under that bridge.
And started climbing the tree after that
Little Squirrel.

84

SODY SALLYRYTUS

Little Squirrel went *higher* . . . and *higher* . . .
And the Old Bear came . . . *higher* . . . and *higher* . . .

Little Squirrel went *higher* . . . and *higher* . . .
And the Old Bear came . . . *higher* . . . and *higher* . . .

Clear to the very *tip top* of that tree.

Little Squirrel climbed out on a long limb . . .
Old Bear climbed right out *after* him.

Little Squirrel looked around . . .
he was so *frightened* . . .
and he gave a LEAP . . . into the *next* tree.

Old Bear looked *down* at the ground . . .
He looked *over* at that tree . . .
And Old Bear said:

> "HUMPF!
> If HE can jump it with them little legs of *his* . . .
> why *I* can jump it
> with these BIG LEGS OF MINE!"

And HE gave a jump!

And *you* know what happened to HIM!

He fell *right* down to the ground . . .
busted wide open . . .
and almost killed him DEAD . . . but not QUITE.

And when he busted open . . .
why out came the Old Lady . . .
and the Old Man . . .
and the Little Girl . . .
and the Little Boy . . .
and they weren't *hurt* at all
because he'd swallowed them *whole*, you know . . .

And the Old Lady said:
        "WHERE'S my SODY SALLYRYTUS!??"

And Little Boy said:
        "*Here* it is,"
and *gave* it to her.

Then she took out a needle and thread she had
and *sewed* that Old Bear up
till he was almost good as *new*.

She said:
        "Old BEAR.
        You go away from these woods
        and don't you come back in these parts
        NO MORE."

Old Bear got up on his feet.
He said:
        "HUMPF!!!"

Walked off
and didn't come *back* no more.

86

SODY SALLYRYTUS

They went along home
and the Old Woman made a big batch of biscuits
and they ate and they ate
till they couldn't eat any more
and the *pet squirrel*
ate the *most* of *all.*

Them biscuits made out of
SODY SALLYRYTUS!!!

NOTES ON TELLING:

I love to tell this tale in my own southern Indiana dialect; "walking" becomes "*walkin.*'" My bear exclaims "By
CRACKY! I'm goin' to eat you up!" or "By GUMMY! I'm
goin' to eat you up," varying his expletive every time a new
victim approaches. When my bear falls from the tree "It PERT-
NEAR killed him dead, but not QUITE." I have removed
such colloquialisms from the text for this book. The tale is
delightful in dialect but need not be told that way. Just tell
it in your own idiom.

Virginia Tashjian includes this tale in her *Juba This
and Juba That* as an audience-participation tale. She suggests
saying the "I'll eat you up" lines in unison. Personally, I find
that this tale works best without the audience participation.
There is such dramatic intensity in this story that the audience
seems to want to be told what the old bear said. I attack the
"WHO'S that walkin' over my bridge?!!" with a great pounce
that makes them squeal. Although I don't use audience participation during the story, I do pause at the end to let them all

join me on the last line, SODY SALLYRYTUS. It comes out like a satisfied sigh.

After this story has been told a time or two, the children will want to act it out. On repeated tellings I might turn to one member of the audience and address him personally, "Old Man, would you go down to the store?" The more active child will often leap to his feet and set out across the stage at once, seizing his moment in the limelight without any further direction from me.

Connie Regan has added a "Sody Salleratus" traveling song to her rendition of the tale and includes considerable audience participation in her telling. You may hear her performance on the Western Woods recording "The Folktellers: Tales to Grow On (WW711, 1981)."

Try the story with and without audience participation and find a style that suits you best.

COMPARATIVE NOTES

Richard Chase includes "Sody Sallyrytus" in his *Grandfather Tales* (p. 75-80). Chase cites his source as Kena Adams of Wise County, Virginia. He states that he has elaborated the tale based on his own use of the story with children. I have done the same. Chase's tale ends with the bear's busting open and spilling out all the people. I became so attached to the old bear, however, that I just have him sewn up again and sent on his way. My bear's comment as he walks off comes from a strange bit of a tale told me often by my father when I was a child. A bear was walking along in the forest when he found a soap box overturned on the ground. The bear walked around it, snuffed around it, and finally raised it up and looked under it. My father always ended the tale like this: "The bear said 'HMPH! No SOAP!' And fell over dead." This story never made a bit of sense to me, but my father kept on telling it and I loved to hear it. Anyway, that's why MY bear gets sewed back up, says "HUMPH!" and walks off. I guess

I always did want that bear to get back up again. In most cases I speak strongly against tampering with tale motifs, but there are exceptions!

The tale's beginning is a variant of Type 122E *Wait for the fat goat (Three Billy Goats Gruff)*. The Aarne-Thompson tale type index lists Norwegian, Swedish, Hungarian, and Indian variants of this tale.

MacDonald's *Storyteller's Sourcebook* lists "Three Billy Goats Gruff" under K533.2 *Wait for the fat goat*. Sody Sallyrytus is indexed in MacDonald under Z33.1 *The fat cat*. Although the tale is structured after "Three Billy Goats Gruff, it soon becomes closely related to "The Fat Cat" as the bear eats up one person after another until he finally bursts and all go free. "The Fat Cat," "The Cat and the Parrot," and "Kuratko the Terrible" are variants of this tale familiar to storytellers. MacDonald lists Scandinavian, Indian, Czechoslovakian, and Russian variants of the Z33.1 motif.

Carl Withers in *I Saw a Rocket Walk a Mile* (p. 24-26) gives a closely related variant in which a greedy old man eats up a pot of mush, a barrel of milk, a boy, a girl, a dog, chases a squirrel up a tree, imitates squirrel's fall, and bursts. Withers took the tale from Walter A. Barnes, *West Virginia Folklore*, v. 3 (p. 2-3).

See the Comparative Notes under "The Little Rooster and the Turkish Sultan" in this book for more discussion of Z33.1 and related motifs.

TURKEY TALE

1. Once there was an old man and an old woman who lived in a round sod house.

2. by the side of a large round lake.

3. The house had one tiny window.

4. Near the lake were two tents.

5. Every day the folks who lived in the tents would walk up the path to the lake to fetch water.

Each tent had a path to the lake.

6. Every day the old woman would walk down to the lake to fetch water.

7. In the lake were many fish.

8. On the lake were many ducks.

9. One day when the old woman walked down to the lake she saw a strange sight. It looked like this!

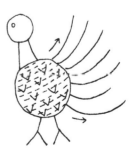

10.   "Husband! Husband!" she called.
"Look out of the window!
The fish are all flying away from the lake!"

Her husband stuck his nose out of the window.

He said "Wife, you silly goose.
Those weren't *fish*.
Those were the *birds* flying away from the lake.

And I do believe you have found the biggest
bird of all.
Just the thing for our
THANKSGIVING dinner.

It's a TURKEY!"

TALE NOTES

This is a draw-as-you-tell story. Pause at the end and show the picture around so most of the audience can guess what it is before you name it.

An interesting African variant of this tale is given in William Stevenson's *The Bushbabies* (p.198-199). The bird drawn is a stork, the tail feathers are formed by a leak in the dam.

American variants of this tale appear in Laura Ingalls Wilder's *On the Banks of Plum Creek* (p. 318) and in Carl Withers' *The Wild Ducks and the Goose*. Withers cites Clifton Johnson's *The Birch-Tree Fairy Book* as his source, and mentions also two versions in *The Journal of American Folk-lore* (X, 1897, p. 323, and XI, 1898, p. 76).

I changed the goose-stork-duck to a turkey in order to use this as a Thanksgiving tale.

See also Anne Pellowski, *The Story Vine*, p. 52 for other drawing tales and comparative notes.

94

JACK AND THE ROBBERS

Once there was a boy named Jack
and he went out to *seek his fortune.*

Jack went along...
and he went along...
and he went along...
till he met a *cat.*

> The cat said "MEOW...MEOW...MEOW...
> Where are you *going* Jack?"
>
> "I'm off to seek my *fortune,*" said Jack.
>
> "Can I go with you?"
>
> "CERTAINLY!" said Jack.
> "COME ALONG!"

And off they went.
Jigglety-jolt...jigglety-jolt...jigglety-jolt...

Till they met a *dog.*

> The dog said, "WOOF...WOOOF...WOOOF...
> Where are you *going* Jack?"
>
> "I'm off to scck my *fortune,*" said Jack.

"Can I go with you?"

"CERTAINLY!" said Jack.
"COME ALONG!"

And off they went.
Jigglety-jolt...jigglety-jolt...jigglety-jolt...

Till they met a *goat.*

The goat said, "BAAA...BAAA...BAAA...
Where are you *going* Jack?"

"I'm off to seek my *fortune,*" said Jack.

"Can I go with you?"

"CERTAINLY!" said Jack.
"COME ALONG!"

And off they went.
Jigglety-jolt...jigglety-jolt...jigglety-jolt...

Till they met a *bull.*

The bull said "BAAWWWL...BAAWWWL...
BAAWWWL...
Where are you *going* Jack?"

"I'm off to seek my *fortune,*" said Jack.

"Can I go with you?"

"CERTAINLY!" said Jack.
"COME ALONG!"

And off they went.
Jigglety-jolt...jigglety-jolt...jigglety-jolt...

Till they met a *cock*.

The cock said, "COCK-A-DOODLE-DOOOO...
COCK-A-DOODLE-DOOOO...
COCK-A-DOODLE-DOOOO...
Where are you *going* Jack?"

"I'm off to seek my *fortune*," said Jack.

"Can I go with you?"

"CERTAINLY!" said Jack.
"COME ALONG!"

And off they went.
Jigglety-jolt...jigglety-jolt...jigglety-jolt...

Jigglety-jolt...jigglety-jolt...jigglety-jolt...
Jigglety-jolt...jigglety-jolt...jigglety-jolt...
...UP the hill...and DOWN the hill...
and THROUGH the valley...
...UP the hill...and DOWN the hill...
and THROUGH the valley...

...UP the hill...and DOWN the hill...
  and THROUGH the valley...
till it came down *dark*.

"Where shall we *sleep?*" said the animals.

"Leave that to *me*," said Jack.

On the hill Jack saw a house.
Jack climbed the hill and *spied* in the window.
Jack saw *three robbers* sitting there
counting out their *gold*.

"My *fortune* is *made*," said Jack.

Jack called the animals.

"Here's what we'll do."

Jack put the bull by the window.
Jack put the goat on the bull's back.
Jack put the dog on the goat's back.
Jack put the cat on the dog's back.
Jack put the cock on the cat's back.

When they were all ready Jack said:
  "When I give the signal...
    you all make the MOST FEROCIOUS noise you
    know how to make!"

When Jack gave the signal

the bull began to "baawwlll..."
the goat began to "baaaa..."
the dog began to "wooofff..."
the cat began to "meow..."
and the cock began to cry
  "COCK-A-DOODLE-DOOOO..."

Such a NOISE!

The three robbers were *terrified*!
They looked out the window and they saw an *animal*
  that was
part BULL-part GOAT-part DOG-part CAT- and
  part COCK!
It was TERRIFYING!

The robbers *threw* their money in the air.
They ran *out* the door and down the hill
and they never came *back*.

Jack and the animals went into the house
and counted out the gold.
There was a bag of gold for everyone.

There was a bag for the bull,
a bag for the goat,
a bag for the dog,
a bag for the cat,
a bag for the cock,
and *Jack* had the biggest bag of all.

So next morning off they went back home
  the way they had come.

Jigglety-jolt...jigglety-jolt...jigglety-jolt...
...UP the hill...and DOWN the hill...
  and THROUGH the valley...
...UP the hill...and DOWN the hill...
  and THROUGH the valley...
...UP the hill...and DOWN the hill...
  and THROUGH the valley...
Jigglety-jolt...jigglety-jolt...jigglety-jolt...
Till they came home RICH.

NOTES ON TELLING

This old favorite works well as an audience participation tale with pre-school or primary-grade children. Warm the
audience up by letting them decide what noises they wish to
make for each animal to be encountered. Let them chime in
as each animal is met. Cue them with the line "And the *cat*
said. . . . ????" The audience responds with a cacophony of
meowing. Let the audience walk with Jack by slapping their
hands lightly on their thighs as he "went along . . . and went
along . . ." and "Jigglety-jolt . . . jigglety-jolt. . . ." After he has
met all of the animals, I carry on an extended "jigglety-jolting"
journey with hand motions "Up the hill and Down the hill
and Through the valley" as we travel through the day. When
the animals give their ferocious roar to frighten the robbers,
I let each child make the sound of one animal. I stop the story
briefly at this point and tell them to decide which animal they
are going to represent. On the count of three we all begin to
bellow, bleat, bark, meow, and crow. It can also be fun to

100

break the group into bulls, goats, etc. and let each section make one animal sound. This requires assigning sections and practicing, and makes a more serious break in the flow of the story than the first technique suggested.

As we travel back I let the jigglety-jolts at the tale's end become fainter and fainter until we arrive in silence at the tale's ending line.

Though my tale is patterned after Veronica Hutchinson's *Candle-Light Stories* (p. 107-113) in its simplicity, I draw my inspiration for the tale from Richard Chase's filmed telling "Jack and the Robbers" and tell the tale in my own southern Indiana dialect as a "Jack" tale.

COMPARATIVE NOTES

"Jack and the Robbers" is a variant of Type 130 *Animals in Night Quarters (Bremen City Musicians)*. Motifs are B296 *Animals go-a-journeying* and K335.1.4 *Animals climb on one another's backs and cry out: frighten robbers*.

The "Bremen Town Musicians" is a favorite tale in children's collections. Under K335.1.4 *MacDonald's Storyteller's Sourcebook* cites 23 children's sources for the Grimm's tale, plus variants from Belgium, Pakistan, Puerto Rico, Scotland, and Yugoslavia.

Aarne-Thompson's tale type index cites variants as: Livonian, Lappish, Swedish, Norwegian, Danish, Scottish, Irish, French, Spanish, Dutch, Flemish, Walloon, German, Italian, Rumanian, Slovenian, Serbocroatian, Polish, Russian, Greek, Turkish, Japanese, Franco-American, English-American, Spanish-American, West Indian, American Negro, African.

Aarne-Thompson lists the following sub-types of the tale: Type 130A *animals build themselves a house*; Type 130B *Animals in flight after threatened death*; Type 130C *Animals in* company of man; Type 130D *Animals warm themselves.* "Jack and the Robbers" is Type 130C *Animals in company of man.* MacDonald's *Storyteller's Sourcebook* indexes this tale as K335.1.4.2★ and cites four English and three Irish variants. Richard Chase's "Jack and the Robbers" (*Jack Tales*, p. 40-46) gives an Appalachian variant.

All of the Type 130 tales follow a similar pattern. An animal, or man, leaves home, picks up traveling companions on the way, routs robbers from a house (sometimes by perching the animals on each other's back and making a row) and takes possession of the house. The tale sometimes is told in conjunction with K1161.1 *Animals hidden in various parts of house attack owners with their characteristic powers.* The animals hide in carefully arranged corners of the house and attack a robber sent to scout out the situation. He perceives them to be a gang armed with axes (goat's horns), awls (cat's claws), etc. and thinks the rooster on the roof is calling "Cook him in the stew" or some such threat. He flees.

This K1161.1 motif often occurs independent of the K335.1.4 *Animals climb on one another's back* motif. MacDonald lists Norwegian and Russian tales in which the animals build a house, then rout a wolf.

Closely related is Type 210 *Cock, hen, duck, pin, and needle on a journey.* MacDonald indexes this as K1161.7★, which includes not only the Grimm tales "Mr. Korbes" and "The Good for Nothings" but also Bulgarian and New Mexican variants in which the animals go on a journey, hide in a house or inn, and rout a villain.

In a widespread Asian variant an old woman routs an unwanted intruder by placing a needle, dung, exploding eggs, crabs, and other items in strategic places about her home. MacDonald lists as K1161.3★+ variants from China, Pakistan, India, and Korea. In a Burmese variant Thumbling defeats an ogre; Japanese variants show Crab defeating Monkey: a Korean variant has a young man besting a tiger.

Other variants include an Uncle Remus tale in which Brer Terrapin falls from a shelf onto Brer Fox's head and Brer Rabbit spits tobacco juice in the fox's eyes when he looks up the chimney. A Russian variant finds Grandpa rescuing Grandma and grandchildren from Old Verlooka with the help of animals and objects hidden in the house. In Venezuela, Juan Bobo routs Tiger, Onion in the stew flies in Tiger's eyes and Vine grips him.

A discussion of Type 130 and a listing of variants appears in Clarkson and Cross *World Folktales* (p. 156-158). Richard Chase cites several scholarly sources for further variants and discussion of Type 130 in his *Jack Tales* (p. 191). Those who read German may wish to consult Antti Aarne's study of this tale, "Die Tiere auf der Wanderschaft" *Folklore Fellows Communications XI*.

ROLY POLY RICE BALL

In Japan
there once lived a kind old man and his wife.
Right next door
lived a greedy old man and his wife.

One day the kind old man went off to work
   in his fields.
He was very poor.
All his wife could give him for his lunch
were three rice balls.
She wrapped them in a furoshiki cloth
and he went off to work.

As the old man was walking along
one of the rice balls suddenly rolled out
   of the cloth
and began to roll along the ground!
      "Koro . . . koro . . . koro . . ."

     "Stop, Little Rice Ball
     Come back!" called the kind old man.

He ran after the rice ball
but PLOP
the rice ball rolled into a hole in the ground!
"Koro . . . koro . . . koro . . ."

The old man bent over . . .
he *looked* down into the hole . . .

Tiny voices were calling:
"Roly Poly Rice Ball
Roll right IN!
Roly Poly Rice Ball
Roll right IN!"

"How *unusual!*" thought the kind old man.

He took out his second rice ball
and rolled *it* down the hole.
"Koro . . . koro . . . koro . . ."

Then he listened . . .

"Roly Poly Rice Ball
Roll right IN!
Roly Poly Rice Ball
Roll right IN!"

"AMAZING!" said the kind old man.

He took out his last rice ball
and rolled *it* down the hole after the others.
"Koro . . . koro . . . koro . . ."

"Roly Poly Rice Ball
Roll right IN!
Roly Poly Rice Ball
Roll right IN!"

"This is indeed *strange*," said the kind old man.

He took his furoshiki and rolled it into a neat ball.
Then the old man rolled the furoshiki down the hole.
"Koro . . . koro . . . koro . . ."

"Roly Poly furoshiki
Roll right IN!
Roly Poly furoshiki
Roll right IN!"

The old man *leaned* over the hole . . .
He *looked* down into the dark hole . . .

"Roly Poly OLD MAN
Roll right IN!
Roly Poly OLD MAN
Roll right IN!"

The old man felt himself slipping and sliding,
then head-over-heels.
He somersaulted *down* into the hole!

"Koro . . . koro . . . koro . . . koro. . . ."

The old man landed with a PLOP
He sat up and looked around.

ROLY POLY RICE BALL

The old man had landed in MOUSE COUNTRY,
the tiny land under the earth where mice
  sing and play.

 Little lady mice, wearing beautiful kimonos
   were singing and dancing.
Little men mice were pounding rice in a tiny rice
   mortar while they too sang.

    "When the cat is far away
    flowers will bloom
    flowers will bloom
    in the mouse country
    the mouse country. . . ."

The little mice *bowed* to the kind old man.
    "Thank you old man,
    for the *rice balls.*
    We will *dance* for you."

The lady mice began to dance and
   then to sing in their high little mouse voices.

    "When the cat is far away
    flowers will bloom
    flowers will bloom
    in the mouse country . . ."

The men mice pounded their rice
   and sang in their lowest mouse voices.

"When the cat is far away
flowers will bloom
flowers will bloom
in the mouse country . . ."

"How lovely! How lovely!" cried the kind old man

"What a *kind* old man you are," said the mice.
"Come and eat with us."

They set before the old man all sorts of delicious
    foods to eat.
There were rice cakes,
    chestnuts and persimmons, fresh fish,
    and round, ripe peaches.

"Oh," said the kind old man.
"If only we had food like this at home.
My wife and I are so poor we have only plain
    white rice to eat."

"Old man we will give you a *gift*," said the mice.
"Take this golden hammer.
Whenever you feel hungry,
just give the hammer a shake.
You shall see!"

And they gave the old man a *tiny* golden hammer.

When the old man had thanked the mice
he crawled back up the mouse hole
and hurried home to his wife.

108

ROLY POLY RICE BALL

"Look what the *mice* have given me!"

The kind old woman took the little hammer,
she shook it.
The table *filled* with good things to eat!

"We will never be hungry again,"
said the kind old man.

And they never were.

But the greedy old man next door
heard about the magic hammer.

"I will go to the mice
and get an even *better* hammer,"
he said.

The greedy old man took three rice balls
and hurried off to find the hole to the mouse country.

There it WAS!

The greedy old man threw a rice ball down the hole.

He didn't hear singing.
He threw another rice ball
and another. . .

Still he heard no singing.

So he impatiently sang out himself.

"Old Man, Old Man
Roll right IN!"

Then he rolled *himself* right down the hole
into the MOUSE COUNTRY.

"Koro . . . koro . . . koro . . . koro. . . ."

Now the mice had not *invited* the greedy old man.
They did not notice him rolling in.
He hid behind a tree and watched the little mice
   with greedy eyes.

They were singing and dancing delicately

"When the cat is far away
flowers will bloom
flowers will bloom
in the mouse country . . ."

Suddenly the Old Man had an idea.
From behind his tree he called loudly
"MEOW!!! MEOW!!!"

The tiny mice scampered away in terror.

"Help . . . help . . . the CAT is here!"

When the mice had all fled
the greedy old man looked around until he found
   a tiny golden hammer.

110

"Here is my *treasure*," he said to himself.

Taking the hammer, he crawled back up the mouse
  hole
and went home to his greedy wife.

"Shake the HAMMER! . . . Shake it!"
said the greedy old man.

His wife *shook* the tiny hammer over the table.

At once the table filled with
mud . . . slime . . . spiders . . . slugs . . .
every imaginable sort of horrid thing.

That was the greedy old man's reward.

From far away it seemed that tiny voices
  could be heard singing.

"When the cat is far away
flowers will bloom
flowers will bloom
in the Mouse Country
the Mouse Country. . ."

NOTES ON TELLING

Japanese folk tales are full of delightful onomatapoeic
words. The audience may want to join in the "koro . . . koro

... koro ... koro ..." as the rice balls roll down the hole. Elizabeth Scofield, whose *Hold Tight, Stick Tight* was the main inspiration for this tale, is careful to include the original Japanese onomatapoeic phrases in her stories. These make her collections especially useful for tellers.

Children will want to join in on the "Roly Poly Rice Ball" chant. You may even want to make up a little tune and sing the rice ball in. Or you could use the Japanese chant "Onigiri, Koro Rin! Koro Rin!" which means "Rice ball, roll in! roll in!"

When telling to pre-schoolers, I let them rise and dance with me as the mouse maidens perform. We wave tiny imaginary fans and sway gracefully as we sing. Then we take up our rice-pounding mallets and sing in a lower mouse man voice as we pound our rice on the second chorus. The mallets are as big as sledge hammers and the men mice take turns pounding in rhythm in a huge mortar. See the illustration in Scofield's book if you are unclear of the imagery. I was unable to locate a Japanese source for the song's score, so I made up my own.

After the storytime, my pre-schoolers make folded paper fans. Then we re-enact the mouse maidens' dance, letting one child be the cat. The cat hides while the mice sing and dance, then pounces! All the mice scamper for cover.

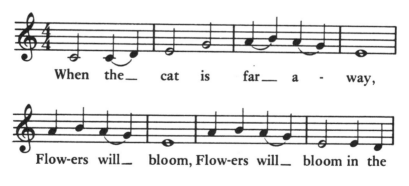

When the__ cat is far__ a - way,

Flow-ers will__ bloom, Flow-ers will__ bloom in the

mouse coun - try, The mouse coun - try.

COMPARATIVE NOTES

This story appears in Elizabeth Scofield's *Hold Tight, Stick Tight* (p. 40-46), in Florence Sakade's *Japanese Children's Stories* (p. 60-73), and in Junichi Yoda's picture book *The Rolling Rice Ball*. MacDonald's *Storyteller's Sourcebook* lists these variants as Motif N777.0.3* based on Thompson's N777 *Dropped ball (basket) leads to adventure when recovery is attempted*.

A related Japanese tale (MacDonald N777.0.2) finds an old man following a dumpling down a hole to encounter a statue of Jizo, the patron deity of travelers. The man hides on the Jizo's head and routs gambling ogres by crowing, not unlike the Bremen Town Musicians. The mean old man next door imitates. (Claus Stamm, *The Dumplings and the Demons*, Yoshiko Uchida, *The Magic Listening Cap*, p. 123-131.)

In another Japanese tale (MacDonald N777.0.1) an old woman follows a dumpling or a rice ball down a hole into another country. She passes Jizos and reaches the home of the Oni (ogres). She cooks for them, but manages to escape with their magic rice paddle; they drink up the river but she makes them laugh and spit back the water (Lafcadio Hearn. *The Boy Who Drew Cats*). MacDonald lists four other sources for the Hearn version, as well as Betsy Bang, *The Goblin's Giggle* and Arlene Mosel, *The Funny Little Woman*.

Japanese folklore contains many stories about the kind old man and the mean old man next door. Scofield's *Hold Tight, Stick Tight* contains six tales on this theme. Keigo Seki's *Folktales of Japan* includes several good-man bad-man tales in the section "Kindness Rewarded and Evil Punished." Good-man bad-man tales familiar to children may include "The Old Man Who Made Cherry Trees Blossom" (MacDonald D1571.1), "The Tongue-Cut Sparrow" (MacDonald Q285.1.1), and "The Old Man with the Wens" (MacDonald F344.1+). Other well-known examples are Type 565 *Why the sea is salt* (MacDonald D1651.3.1, A1115.2.1) and Type 834 *The poor brother's treasure* (MacDonald N182+). In *The Poor Brother's*

Treasure a good man finds treasure, a bad neighbor imitates and finds filth. He drops the filth down the chimney of the good man and it turns to gold.

For additional good-man bad-man tales see MacDonald references under J2415 *Foolish imitation of lucky man.* Note also the similarity of these tales to the kind and unkind girl tales (Type 480, MacDonald Q2.1+).

UDALA TREE

There was an orphan boy
who had no mother or father of his own.
He lived with his stepmother
and two stepbrothers.

Now whenever there was food to be had
the stepmother and the stepbrothers ate the good food
and gave the orphan boy only the scraps.

Whenever there was *work* to be done
the stepmother and the stepbrothers
   would do only the lightest work
and give all the hardest work to the Boy.

Every day he had to sweep the compound,
hoe the garden,
and bring water from the river.

One day when the Boy was sweeping the compound
he found the seed of an Udala tree
lodged in a crack in the ground.

The Boy owned *nothing* of his own.
He thought I will *keep* this shiny Udala seed.
It will be something that *belongs to me.*

That night when the Boy slept
he put the Udala seed under his pillow.
And while he slept he had a *dream.*

The Boy dreamed that an Udala tree
grew from the tiny seed under his pillow
and spread its branches over his head.

The next morning
the Boy took the Udala seed to the garden.
He made a tiny hole and planted the seed.
He covered it over. . . .
He brought water from the stream and watered it.

Then the Boy sat down
and he began to chant.

     "Udala GROW!
     NDA!

Udala GROW!
NDA!
Grow for motherless child!
NDA!
Grow for fatherless Child!
NDA!
The Earth is a place of call.
NDA!
Man stops here and goes on."

And as the Boy chanted
a tiny shoot began to grow from the Udala seed.

The Boy chanted louder.

"Udala GROW!
NDA!
Udala GROW!
NDA!
Grow for motherless child!
NDA!
Grow for fatherless child!
NDA!
The Earth is a place of call.
NDA!
Man stops here and goes on.
NDA!"

And as the Boy chanted
the *Udala* tree began to grow . . .
it grew taller than the Boy's head.

The Boy became EXCITED!

> "Udala GROW!
> NDA!
> Udala GROW!
> NDA!
> Grow for motherless child!
> NDA!
> Grow for fatherless child!
> NDA!
> The Earth is a place of call.
> NDA!
> Man stops here and goes on.
> NDA!"

Before his very eyes
that seed grew until it became a great Udala tree.
And spread its branches over his head.

The Boy sat in the shade of his *very own* Udala tree.
And he was *happy*.

Then the Boy thought
"What if the tree should bear *fruit?*"

So the Boy chanted:

> "Udala FRUIT!
> NDA!
> Udala FRUIT!
> NDA!
> Fruit for motherless child!

NDA!
Fruit for fatherless child!
NDA!
The Earth is a place of call.
NDA!
Man stops here and goes on.
NDA!"

Then over his head
Udala fruit grew on the branches.
Tiny green Udala fruit covered the tree.

The Boy chanted for the fruit to *ripen*.

"Udala RIPEN!
NDA!
Udala RIPEN!
NDA!
Ripen for motherless child!
NDA!
Ripen for fatherless child!
NDA!
The Earth is a place of call.
NDA!
Man stops here and goes on.
NDA!"

All through the Udala tree
the fruit turned a ripe yellowish brown.

But the Boy could not reach the fruit.
He called for the fruit to . . . *drop*.

"Udala DROP!
NDA!
Udala Drop!
NDA!
Drop for motherless child!
NDA!
Drop for fatherless child!
NDA!
The Earth is a place of call.
NDA!
Man stops here and goes on.
NDA!"

All about the Boy
in his lap
on the ground
all around the tree
fell the *ripe Udala fruit.*

The Boy *ate* of the delicious Udala fruit.
Never had he been so full.
Never had he felt so contented.

In the evening the stepmother and stepbrothers
returned from the village.
They saw the tall Udala tree in their garden
and were astonished.

The Boy told them to pick whatever of the Udala
fruit they wanted
from the ground.

But he warned them *never to touch*
his magic Udala tree.
They must never *climb* the tree
or *pick* the fruit.

The stepmother and stepbrothers ate of the delicious
fruit and were delighted.

Some days later
when the Boy was hoeing the garden
he heard a noise in his tree.
The two stepbrothers had climbed the Udala tree
and were breaking the branches
to get at the fruit!

The Orphan Boy was FURIOUS!

He began to chant for the tree to grow
   higher into the air
carrying the two boys with it.

> "Udala GROW!
> NDA!
> Udala GROW!!
> NDA!
> *GROW!* For motherless child!
> NDA!
> *GROW!* For fatherless child!
> NDA!
> The Earth is a place of call!
> NDA!
> Man stops here and goes on!
> NDA!"

The stepbrothers began to scream for *help*.

Their mother ran from the house.
She *begged* the Orphan Boy to stop the tree.

But he was *angry*
and he *would not*.

He chanted for the tree to grow *taller*
into the sky.

> "UDALA GROW!!!
> NDA!
> UDALA GROW!!!
> NDA!
> GROW!! For MOTHERLESS child!
> NDA!
> GROW!! For FATHERLESS child!
> NDA!
> The Earth is a place of call!
> NDA!
> Man stops here and goes on!
> NDA!"

And the tree grew taller. . .
taller . . .
taller . . .
until the boys disappeared
into the clouds.

122

The villagers ran to see this strange thing.
then the stepmother . . .
before all the assembled villagers . . .
promised to give the Boy
only the *best food* to eat
only the *lightest* WORK to do
if he would bring back her sons.

When the Boy heard her make this promise
before the entire village
he knew she would have to keep her promise.
And so he relented.

He called for the tree to *shrink*.

And slowly
the tree shrank back toward the earth
until it was its normal size again
and the boys were able to climb back to the ground.

From that day
the Orphan Boy
was given only the *best* food
and only the *lightest* labor
in that household.

And always . . .
always . . .
that Boy remembered to share with everyone
the fruit of his
MAGIC UDALA TREE.

NOTES ON TELLING

Before beginning the tale, we rehearse calling "NDA!" as we clap our hands. Throughout the story the audience joins in the response by simultaneously clapping and calling "NDA!" after each line of the refrain. Our "NDA!" becomes increasingly vociferous as the angry boy takes vengeance on his stepbrothers.

I chose Uche Okeke's version of this tale as a primary source for my own telling because I like the philosophical phrase "The earth is a place of call . . . man stops here and goes on . . ." in his refrain. As he does not give musical notation for this song, I simply chant it.

COMPARATIVE NOTES

My telling is taken mainly from Uche Okeke's *Tales of Land of Death: Igbo Folk Tales*. The tale's philosophical phrase "The earth is a place of call . . . man stops here and goes on . . ." does not appear in either of the other versions I have seen. Though Okeke implies that this is a song, he gives no score. Adjai Robinson gives a variant of this tale "The Stepchild and the Fruit Trees" in his *Singing Tales of Africa* (p. 24-33). He includes musical notation and text for the song. The tale also appears in Diane Wolkstein's *The Magic Orange Tree and other Haitian Tales* (Knopf, 1978, p. 13-22). Wolkstein includes words and music for her song.

In both the Robinson and Wolkstein variants, the protagonist is a girl child, bringing the tale closer to the European Cinderella tradition. In the German variant, "Aschenputtle," a tree grows from the dead mother's grave bearing clothes for the orphaned girl. (See MacDonald's *Storyteller's Sourcebook* R221B.) MacDonald also lists Finnish (R221N), American Indian (R221G), and Italian (R221C) Cinderella variants, which all include a treasure-bearing tree. A Ceylonese variant, "Blue Lotus Flower," which appears in Ruth Tooze's *The Wonderful*

Wooden Peacock Flying Machine and Other Tales of Ceylon (p. 77-82), is even closer to the African/Caribbean tale. A wicked aunt kills a white turtle that is the spirit of the girl's mother, and a mango tree grows from the turtle's bones. Only the girl can pick the fruit. The aunt burns the tree but in its place a cucumber vine grows, which again only the girl can pick. The aunt destroys the vine, which is replaced by a blue lotus. The girl picks the lotus for the king, who marries her.

Both Okeke and Wolkstein include a "stretching tree" motif. This is related to Thompson F54.1 *Tree stretching to sky (Jack and the beanstalk, et al)*; K111.3 *Abandonment on stretching tree (tricked into climbing)*; D1487.3 *Magic spell makes tree grow (beneficial growth)*; D1576.1 *Magic song causes tree to rise to sky*; and D482 *Transformation: Stretching tree. A tree magically shoots upward.*

MacDonald lists several tales with vengeful growth under D482.1. An Australian Aborigine tale tells of a vengeful crow that asks the Tuckonie elves to sing a tree up, carrying the nest of baby pelicans out of their mother's reach. A woodpecker is the rescuer (MacDonald D482.1.1). A similar California Miwok tale has a crow singing up a rock that carries two bluebird brothers. A measuring worm performs the rescue (MacDonald D482.4.1). In a Pueblo tale a jealous companion causes the tree on which a rainmaker sits to grow to the sky. There is no rain until the tree is lowered (MacDonald D482.1.3).

In Okeke's tale two stepbrothers are carried to the sky, while their mother begs for their return. Wolkstein's version has the wicked stepmother herself carried up by the tree and destroyed when the girl chants for the tree to break. Robinson's version reaches a denouement by having the girl sing for her tree to die. When the stepmother, who claims the tree is hers, is unable to revive it in front of the villagers, the girl is proved rightful owner.

THE RABBIT AND THE WELL

Once a drought
came to the forest.
It didn't rain for a long, long time.
The animals had no water to drink.
All the streams dried up.
All the ponds dried up.
There was no water anywhere for the animals to drink.

The animals held a meeting in the forest.
They said:

> "We will have to *dig a well*.
> *Everyone* must help."

All of the animals said they would help.
All *except* Mister Rabbit.

126

THE RABBIT AND THE WELL

"AH . . . CHAA . . ." said Mister Rabbit.
"YOU dig the well
and *I'll* drink the *water*."

"Oh no," said the animals.
"If you don't help dig the well
you can't drink the water."

"AH . . . CHAA . . ." said Mister Rabbit.
"YOU dig the well.
I'll drink the water.

Don't worry."

The animals worked very hard all day.
By evening they had dug a deep well in the forest.
It filled with cool, clear water.
Each animal had a long drink of the water,
then they went away to their beds in the forest.

As soon as it was dark
Mister Rabbit came hopping over the brow of the hill.
He hopped right down to the well . . .
Had himself a long . . . cool . . . drink . . .
and then knocked some *mud* into the water,
left his muddy footprints all around that well,
and hopped off into the briar patch,
which was his home.

Next morning
when the animals came to their well

there were *rabbit* footprints
all around the well.
And someone had *muddied* up the water.

> "It's that pesky rabbit," they said.
> "We'll have to leave someone to guard the well
>   tonight."

So that night they left
Mister Bear
to guard the well.

As soon as it was dark
Mister Rabbit hopped over the brow of the hill.
He saw Mister Bear sitting by the well
so he hid behind a bush.
He thought for a moment
then he began to *sing.*

> "Cha Ra Ra
>   Will ya? Will ya? *Can* ya?
>   Cha Ra Ra
>   Will ya? Will ya? *Can* ya?"

> "Hmmmmmm," said Mister Bear.
> "I hear *music.*
> The animals must be having a dance
> and they didn't invite *me.*
> I'm going to find that dance."

So Mister Bear lumbered off into the forest
looking for the dance.

As soon as he was gone
Mister Rabbit
hopped down to the well.
He had himself a long drink of the cool water.
Then that pesky rabbit
knocked some more *mud* into the well
and left his muddy rabbit footprints
all around the well.

Then he hopped off into his home in the briar patch.

Next morning
when the animals came to the well
There were those rabbit footprints again.

> "We'll have to leave someone SMARTER
> to guard the well tonight," the animals said.
> "Let's leave Mister Monkey.
> He's clever enough."

So that night
when the animals went home to their beds in the forest
they left
Mister Monkey
to guard the well.

As soon as it was dark
Mister Rabbit
came hopping over the brow of the hill.

He saw Mister Monkey
so he hid behind his bush
and he began to sing.

"Cha Ra Ra
Will ya? Will ya? *Can* ya?
Cha Ra Ra
Will ya? Will ya? *Can* ya?"

"Hmmmmmm," said Mister Monkey.
"There's that *music* again.
It's not going to trick *me*.
Now *let me see*.

It can't be the stars in the sky.
It can't be the water in the well.
It must be the *leaves* in the trees!"

And Mister Monkey went off into the forest
looking for those singing leaves.

As soon as he was gone
Mister Rabbit hopped down to the well.
He took his long drink of water . . .
kicked some more mud into the well . . .
stomped his muddy footprints all about . . .
and skipped off to his home in the briar patch.

Next morning
there were those *rabbit footprints* again.
And the well was muddied.

"That rabbit is *too smart* for us,"
said the animals.
"How can we catch him?"

130

Then Mister *Fox* had an idea.

"Let's make a little man
all out of *tar*,"
said Mister Fox.
"We'll put *that* down to guard the well."

So the animals worked very hard
and made a little man
out of sticks
and covered it with sticky, gooey *tar*.

They set that tar man down to guard the well.
Then they all went home to their beds in the forest.

As soon as it was dark
Mister Rabbit
hopped over the brow of the hill.

He saw that tar man sitting there
and he didn't *recognize* him.
He hid behind his bush
and he began to sing.

"Cha Ra Ra
Will ya? Will ya? *Can* ya?
Cha Ra Ra
Will ya? Will ya? *Can* ya?"

The tar man didn't turn around
and didn't say a thing.

"Hmmmm," thought Mister Rabbit.
"Maybe he doesn't hear so well."

Mister Rabbit moved down the hill
a little closer to the tar man.

He sang a little louder.

"CHA Ra Ra!
Will ya? Will ya? CAN YA?
CHA Ra Ra!
Will ya? Will ya? CAN YA?"

Tar man didn't turn around.
He didn't say a thing.

"Hmmmmmm," said Mister Rabbit.
"That old tar man must be very hard of hearing."

He moved right up behind that tar man
and sang as *loud* as he could.

"CHA RA RA!
WILL YA? WILL YA? CAN YA?
CHA RA RA!
WILL YA? WILL YA? CAN YA?"

Tar man didn't turn around.
Tar man didn't move a muscle.

"HEY! You old man.
Don't you like my singing?

132

THE RABBIT AND THE WELL

You'd better ANSWER me when I talk to you.

If you don't ANSWER me
I'm going to give you
a *sock in the snoot*."

Tar man didn't answer.
so Mister Rabbit hauled off and
socked him in the snoot.

And his *fist*
Stuck *tight*
in that *tar.*

> "Oooooooh. You *mean* old man.
> You let go of my fist!
>
> You'd better let go of my FIST!
> Cause if you don't . . .
> I'm gonna sock you with my OTHER fist!"

Tar man didn't let loose.
So Mister Rabbit hauled off
and socked him with his *other* fist.

And *that* fist stuck tight in the tar *too.*

> "Ooooooohhhhh, you mean old man!
> You'd better let go of my FISTS.
>
> Cause if you *don't*
> I'll have to KICK you."

Tar man didn't let go.

So Mister Rabbit *kicked*
that tar man.
And his *foot* stuck tight in the tar.

    "You let go of my foot and my fists.
    If you don't let *go*,
    I'll kick you with my *other* foot I will.
    And kick you HARDER too!"

And Mister Rabbit *kicked* that tar man
with his other foot.
And *that* foot stuck tight in the tar.

Now he was stuck with both feet
and both fists.

Mister Rabbit was *pullin'*
and *hollerin'.*

    "You'd better let go of my feet and my fists!
    If you don't let go of my feet and my fists,
    I'm a-gonna *butt* you with my HEAD I am!"

Mister Rabbit *reared back*
and he BUTTED that old tar man.

And his *head*
stuck tight in that tar.

134

THE RABBIT AND THE WELL

"OH! OH! OH!
YOU MEAN OLD CREATURE YOU!
If you don't let go of my feet and my fists and
    my head right this minute
You're gonna be SORRY!

Because I'm a-gonna BITE YOU!!!"

Mister Rabbit *bit* that tar man.
And his teeth stuck fast in that tar.

Now he was stuck with his fists,
his feet, and his head
and he couldn't even holler for help.

Next morning the animals came to the well
and there was Mister Rabbit
stuck fast to that tar man.

They *pulled* him loose from that tar.

    "What'll we *do* with him?"

Mister Bear said:
    "If I was you
    I'd just *shoot* him."

But when Mister Rabbit heard that
he began to jump up and down and holler:
    "Oh *please* shoot me!
    All my life I've wanted for someone to *shoot* me!
    PLEASE, PLEASE, do shoot me!"

When the animals heard that they said:
    "Why NO.
    If he WANTS us to shoot him
    we won't do THAT."

Mister Fox said:
    "Well then, let's *hang* him."

    "Oh YES YES YES"
    said Mister Rabbit.
    "I've *always* wanted to be hanged."

Everything they would suggest . . .
Mister Rabbit would claim he'd just always wanted
to have that thing done to him.

Finally, they said:
    "Well Mister Rabbit . . .
    Just what *are* you afraid of . . . ?"

Mister Rabbit started *trembling* all over
just like he was scared to death.

    "Oooooohhhhh . . .
    I've always been just *sooo afraid*
    that somebody would put me in a cupboard
    and feed me nothing but cake and ice cream
    until I was so fat I could pop
    and then take me out
    and throw me into that old briar patch over there
    and let me
    BUST.

Oooooohhh . . . I'm so scared of *that*."

"Well that's *just* what we'll do," said the animals.

Mister Bear took his feet.
Mister Fox took his fists.
And they began swinging him back and forth

    "One for the money
    Two for the show
    Three to get ready
    And four . . . to . . . GOOOO!"

And they threw him
higher. . . and higher. . . and higher. . .

And down he started coming
faster. . . and faster. . . and faster. . .

Till he landed with a *plop*
right in the middle of that briar patch.

But he didn't bust.
That briar patch was his *home*.

He ran off through the briar patch calling
    "YIP YIP YIP
      MY NAME'S MOLLY COTTONTAIL
      CATCH ME IF YOU CAN. . . ."

And *they* couldn't catch him.

NOTES ON TELLING

I include this tale despite its length because its repetitious pattern makes it easy to learn. This is an unusual variant of the familiar Tarbaby story. It lacks the dialect of the Joel Chandler Harris version. Never try to tell a story in a dialect that is not absolutely comfortable for you. If parts of this tale feel awkward, rephrase them into language that suits your style better.

I discovered this tale in a 1934 issue of the *Journal of American Folk-Lore* while doing research on the Tarbaby tale. Its unusual ending with the ice cream and cupboard motif seemed charming to me. The peculiar tag ending "My name is Molly Cottontail, Catch me if you Can!" makes no sense at all for a *Mister* Rabbit. But I like its sassy tone and left it in. I keep also the colloquial "Sock you in the SNOOT," which children love.

The key to the whole piece is Mister Rabbit's sassiness. Make his "Ah . . . Chaaa . . ." very sassy. Feel free to make up your own tune for his song, or use mine. I sing in descending tone "Cha, Ra, Ra . . . Will ya . . . Will ya . . . Can YA?" With an upward flip on the final "YA?"

You must decide for yourself whether you prefer to remain still while telling or to act out the characters in a limited way. I usually become involved with a sort of muted action in Mister Rabbit's socking and kicking of the tar man in this tale, and I always act out the "One for the money, two for the show . . ." swing.

This tale can be told with or without audience participation. The children are usually glad to join you in Mr. Rabbit's song. Be sure to start his song sweetly and let his volume increase gradually as he tries to make the tar man notice him.

Cha ra ra-a-a! Will ya? Will ya? Can you?

COMPARATIVE NOTES

This tale is based on a variant published by John Harrington Cox ("Negro Tales from West Virginia," *Journal of American Folklore*, XLVII, 1934, p. 344-347). Cox's version was taken from Dora Lee Newman's version, which she learned from her father, who learned it as a child from "our old Sukey and black Canada." Newman published the tale in a privately printed book *Marion County in the Making*.

"The Rabbit and the Well" is a variant of Type 175, *The tarbaby and the rabbit*, usually associated with Joel Chandler Harris's Uncle Remus stories. There are, however, many African variants of this tale (MacDonald K741) including Swahili (farmer catches hare on sticky scarecrow), Rhodesian (hare caught on sap-covered back of tortoise), West African (elephant catches hare with clay man), Liberian/Ghanian (Anansi spider caught by wife on waxed straw man), Ashanti (Anansi caught stealing food by tar doll), Hausa (Anansi caught by rubber man), Mayagoli (squirrel caught by sticky figure), West African (gum doll set by spider Anansi catches fairy), Yoruba (frog caught by sticky figure), and Nigerian (tortoise caught by tarred clay man).

A Cherokee variant in which rabbit is caught on a tar wolf seems directly related to this tale (Corydon Bell, *John Rattling Gourd of Big Cove*; George P. Scheer, *Cherokee Animal Tales*, p. 47-50). Another Native American tale has a skunk caught on a pine-gum doll by a man (Virginia Haviland, *North American Legends*, p. 71-75). In a Wintu tale from the Sacramento Valley of California, a coyote hits an old alder stump and gets his arms, legs, and head stuck. This tale lacks any trickster motive and is possibly of independent invention.

Folklorists have speculated at length on the possible origins of the Tarbaby tale. Joseph Jacobs finds the fivefold attack motif so "preposterously ludicrous that it cannot have been independently invented" (*Indian Fairy Tales*, p. 306). I wonder. Once you begin attacking a sticky object, the human anatomy makes a fivefold attack imminent!

Jacobs, and other folklorists, have speculated that this

tale had its origins in India. In a Jataka tale, "Prince Five-weapons attacks a Demon-with-Sticky-Hair," the Prince first loses his weapons in the sticky hair and then attacks with hands, feet, and head until he is stuck fast. Buddhist missionaries might have brought this tale to Africa, where the motif has been retold in many forms. Native American variants could have developed after African influences reached America.

The tale is found throughout the world. Aarne-Thompson lists Latvian, French, Spanish, Indian, Japanese, Argentinian, Chilean, Colombian, Cuban, Dominican Republican, Puerto Rican, Venezuelan, Portuguese American, West Indian, Native American, African, and Philippine variants. Thompson adds Angolan, Hottentot, Yoruba, Gold Coast, Kaffir, Ekoi, Mpongwe, Ila, Rhodesian, Cameroon, and Duala variants.

Our children's collections include a Brazilian tale in which monkeys are caught on a wax figure (Rose Dobbs, *Once Upon a Time*, p. 60-66), a Visayan variant in which an ape is caught by a tar man (Elizabeth H. Sechrist, *Once in the First Times*, p. 110-118), an Indonesian variant in which the Giant Gergassi is tricked into a hole covered with rubber latex (Margueritte Bro, *How the Mouse Deer Became King*, p. 72-78), and a Northwest Coast Indian tale in which a captive is lured into a pit using a non-sticky image and a voice thrown through a kelp tube (Christie Harris, *Once Upon a Totem*, p. 89-111).

Another related tale is the Russian "Straw Ox" (MacDonald Z32.4.1). Here several animals are caught on a tarred straw ox. Each rewards the man for releasing it. The motivation for tarring and the result of the capture are unrelated to the K741 Tarbaby motif.

The notion of becoming fast to a sticky object is one which can obviously have widespread independent invention in folktales. A Fijian tale (Anne Gittins, *Tales from the South Pacific Islands*, p. 26-27) tells of an ant stuck to gum on the bark of a breadfruit tree. The ant dies and the tale moves on to other unrelated episodes.

African, American Black, and Native American variants of this tale often continue the tale with motif K581 *Animal "punished" by being placed in favorite environment.* This motif can appear without the Tarbaby attachment, as in the many variants of K581.1, *Drowning punishment for turtle, eel, crab.*

In several instances the Tarbaby motif is introduced with a drought setting—A2233.1.1 *Animals refuse to help dig well, may not drink from river or spring.* MacDonald cites eight variants of K741 which occur in combination with this well motif.

To study this tale further consult the 22 variants cited in MacDonald's *Storyteller's Sourcebook* and see the commentary by Cox in the *Journal of American Folk-lore* Vol XLVII, 1934, p. 342-344. Cox cites several major articles on the Tarbaby tale. Clarkson and Cross (*World Folktales*) also discuss the tale briefly and cite several sources.

HIC! HIC! HIC!*

Once there was
and twice there wasn't.
A very foolish servant boy
whose name was Mustafa.

One day Mustafa's master called him and said:
>"Mustafa, you must go to the market
>and buy me some *salt*.
>Do not forget what you are sent for."

The master knew that Mustafa was very forgetful.

>"Oh no sir," said Mustafa. "I won't forget.
>I will say over and over to myself
>Salt . . . salt . . . salt . . . salt . . .

---

*Pronounced heech.

until I reach the market.
That way I *cannot* forget."

Mustafa set out down the road.

"Salt . . . salt . . . salt . . . salt . . .

But in Mustafa's village in Turkey
salt was called "Hic."

So Mustafa ran off down the road calling
        "Hic . . . Hic . . . Hic . . . Hic . . .
        Hic . . . Hic . . . Hic . . .
        Hic . . . Hic . . . Hic . . . Hic . . .
        Hic . . . Hic . . . Hic."

He was going to say that *all the way* to the market.

On the way he passed over a bridge where a fisherman
    was fishing.
Mustafa stopped to watch the fisherman.

All the while he kept saying:
        "Hic . . . Hic . . . Hic . . . Hic . . .
        Hic . . . Hic . . . Hic."

Now as it happens,
"Hic" can mean "salt"
but it can *also* mean "nothing."

To the fisherman it seemed that Mustafa was saying
"Nothing . . . Nothing . . . Nothing. . . ."

And what do you think that fisherman caught . . . ?

NOTHING!

The fisherman cried:
    "BOY! You should not be *saying* that!"

    "Oh?" said Mustafa.
    "I'm sorry.
    What *should* I be saying?"

    "You should be saying
    'May there be five or TEN of them!
    May there be five or TEN of them!'
    . . . meaning ten big fish!"

    "*Ohhh — I* see." said Mustafa.

    And he ran down the road saying:
    "May there be five or TEN of them!
    May there be five or TEN of them!"

Until he came to where a *funeral procession*
   was passing.
They were carrying a dead man to be buried.

    "May there be five or TEN of them!
    May there be five or TEN of them!"
    said Mustafa.

144

HIC! HIC! HIC!

Everyone turned and began to beat Mustafa.

"Boy! You should not be *saying* that!"

"Ohhh—" said Mustafa.
"I'm sorry.
What *should* I be saying?"

"You should be saying
'May God bless his SOUL . . .
May God bless his SOUL . . .
May God bless his SOUL. . . .'"

"Ohhh—I see."

And Mustafa ran down the road muttering:
"May God bless his SOUL . . .
May God bless his SOUL . . .
May God bless his SOUL . . ."

. . . till he came to where a dead FISH
was lying in the road.
Mustafa stopped to look at the dead fish.

"May God bless his SOUL . . .
May God bless his SOUL . . .
May God bless his SOUL . . ."

Soon a man came by and heard him . . .

"Stop! Stop! Boy!

145

You should not be saying that
to a DEAD FISH!"

"*Ohhh* I'm sorry," said Mustafa.
"What *should* I be saying?"

"You should be saying
'OH what a SMELL
OO what a SMELL!
OH what a SMELL
OO what a SMELL!'" said the man, holding
   his nose.

"*Ohhh — I* see." said Mustafa.

And he ran down the road . . .

"OH what a SMELL . . .
OO what a SMELL . . .
OH what a SMELL . . .
OO what a SMELL . . ."

Until he came to where three lovely ladies . . .
were wearing *very fine* perfume.

"OH what a SMELL . . .
OO what a SMELL . . .
OH what a SMELL . . .
OO what a SMELL . . ." said Mustafa, holding
   his nose.

HIC! HIC! HIC!

The three lovely *ladies*
took off their *slippers*
and began to beat Mustafa over the head.

"BOY! You should not be *saying* that!"

"Ohhhhh . . .
I'm sorry," said Mustafa.
"What *should* I be saying?"

"You should be saying
'Oh how LOVELY . . .
My how NICE . . .
Oh how LOVELY . . .
My how NICE . . . .'
That's what you should be saying."

"Ohhh — *I* see," said Mustafa.

And he hurried down the road . . .

"Oh how LOVELY . . .
My how NICE . . .
Oh how LOVELY . . .
My how NICE . . ."

Until he came to where two men were *fighting*.

When the *first* man hit the *second* man . . .
Mustafa said:
"Oh how LOVELY! . . ."

When the *second* man hit the *first* man . . .
Mustafa said:
    "My how NICE!!!"

Both men stopped fighting
and began to *beat* Mustafa over the head.

    "BOY, you should not be *saying* that!"

    "OOOOOHHHHH . . .
I'm *sorry*.
What *should* I be saying?" said Mustafa.

    "You should be saying
'Please SIRS . . .
Stop FIGHTING good sirs . . .
Please SIRS . . .
Stop FIGHTING good sirs . . .'

That's what you *should* be saying."

    "Ohhh — *I* see."

Mustafa went down the road.

    "Please SIRS . . .
Stop FIGHTING good sirs . . .
Please SIRS . . .
Stop FIGHTING good sirs . . ."

148

HIC! HIC! HIC!

He came to a place where two *dogs* were fighting.
Mustafa stopped to watch the dogfight.
He kept saying:

"Please SIRS . . .
Stop FIGHTING good sirs . . .
Please SIRS . . .
Stop FIGHTING good sirs . . ."

. . . He was saying this to the two *dogs*.

A man heard him and cried:

"Stop! STOP BOY!
You should not be SAYING that!"

"Oooohhh . . . .
I'm sorry . . .
What *should* I be saying? . . ."

"You should be saying
'OUT DOG . . . GET OUT!
OUT DOG . . . GET OUT!'
That's what you say to *dogs*."

"Ohhh — *I* see," said Mustafa.

And he went down the road.

"OUT DOG . . . GET OUT!
OUT DOG . . . GET OUT!"

Until he came to the *market place*.

149

The first shop he came to was the *shoemaker's* shop.
The shoemaker was pulling leather between his teeth
   to stretch it.
Mustafa stopped to watch.

All the while he kept saying

> "OUT DOG . . . GET OUT!
> OUT DOG . . . GET OUT! . . ."

The shoemaker thought he was calling HIM a DOG!
He called:
> "Dog YOURSELF!
> BOY, you should not be *saying* that!"

> "Oooohhh . . ."said Mustafa . . .
> "What *should* I be saying?"

> "YOU . . .
> should say NOTHING!
> Just say 'HIC!'
> That means *NOTHING*."

> "HIC!" cried Mustafa.
> "Hic means *nothing* and 'Hic' means 'SALT'!
> And THAT is what I came to BUY!"

And he ran down the road calling:
> "HIC . . . HIC . . . HIC . . . HIC . . .
> "HIC . . . HIC . . . HIC."

And bought his *salt*.

And went home *very* happy.

NOTES ON TELLING

I include this tale because the repetition makes it easy to learn and to tell. I do not always try for audience participation with this tale, though it can be told that way. The audience is usually glad to chime in on Mustafa's chants as he walks along.

This tale seems to work especially well in fourth grade classes with lots of boys. I usually ask if any of them ever have trouble remembering what they are told to do. They seem to identify with poor Mustafa quite easily.

I use some gesture in the course of the story, such as covering my head in protection as the lovely ladies beat Mustafa about the ears.

See the Comparative Notes for comments on the tale's ending. Perhaps you will find an even better variant.

COMPARATIVE NOTES

This tale is Type 1696 *What should I have said (done)?* The Aarne-Thompson type index lists two Turkish sources for this tale. It also lists sources from India, Indonesia, Africa, Argentina, Chile, Puerto Rico, the United States, and twenty-five European areas. There are French-Canadian and Wyandot variants as well.

Stith Thompson's motif-index subdivides Type 1696 into tales in which the foolish boy (man) does foolish things (J2461) and those in which he says foolish things (J2461.2). One tale often contains both motifs.

The English folk tale "Lazy Jack" is a J2461 tale often included in children's collections. Jack loses his penny and is told to put it in his pocket the next time. Next time he is given milk, etc. MacDonald lists 10 sources for this English tale and variants from Germany, Ireland, Majorca, Portugal, China, Japan, Appalachia, and Jewish and Turkmenian sources.

Our version of "Hic, Hic, Hic" is J2461.2 *Literal following of instructions about greetings. Numbskull gives wrong greeting and is told how to give correct one. When he tries it, however, the conditions are wrong.* MacDonald cites variants of this tale from Switzerland, Portugal, Russia, Majorca, Kashmir, Appalachia, and a Turkmenian source.

Although all of the J2461.2 tales hinge on a foolish person and a misunderstood phrase, Richard Chase's Appalachian tale "Soap, Soap, Soap" seems especially related to our variant (Richard Chase, *Grandfather Tales*, p. 130-136). A little boy sent to buy soap keeps repeating "Soap, Soap, Soap." He falls down, forgets his phrase, and goes off with an inappropriate refrain.

Chase believes that the Appalachian variant is derived from the British tale "Stupid's Cries" (Joseph Jacobs, *More English Folk and Fairy Tales*, p. 195-197). I much prefer the Turkish and Appalachian variants to the British version, however, which runs on through nine episodes and concludes by having the boy condemned to death. The Turkish and Appalachian variants are more concise, and each ties the story up neatly with an episode that reminds the boy of his errand.

Two versions of this Turkish tale are available in children's editions. "The Story of the Boy Who Couldn't Keep Anything in His Head," by Feyyaz Kayacan and Mary Fergar, is found in H. M. Nahmad's *The Peasant and the Donkey: Tales of the Near and Middle East*, p. 123-130). A boy is sent to the market by his grandmother, who tells him to buy "nothing." A vendor at the market informs him that this means "salt." In Barbara K. Walker's picture book *Just Say Hic!*, the boy is sent by his master to fetch "salt" but does not realize that the word "hic" also means nothing. Both stories have weak transitions from the final misinterpreted speech episode to the actual buying of the salt. In the Kayacan/Fergar tale, the boy simply remembers his errand and asks in the marketplace for "nothing." The Walker ending is more effective and is the one I have chosen for my telling. Walker includes an episode with fighting dogs and a final episode with a shoemaker who tells the boy "Just say *hic*!" In other words . . ."*nothing*." Though the shoemaker episode works well, the dogfight episode seems less humorous than the rest of the tale. I suspect that there may be even better variants of this tale, perhaps somewhere in Turkey!

The word "Hic" is taken from the Walker source. She gives the pronunciation as "Heech." This is a good example of the importance of comparing all available variants when preparing a tale for telling, because while the Kayacan/Fergar tale is excellent, the phrase "Hic" and the more effective ending of the Walker variant *improve* the tale.

Clarkson and Cross, *World Folktales*, discuss Type 1696 briefly and list variants (p. 353-355).

MR. FOX

Be Bold Be Bold

Lady Mary was young and Lady Mary was fair.
She had two brothers and more lovers than you could
    count.
But of them all the bravest and most gallant was a
    certain *Mr. Fox* . . .
whom she had met when she was down at her father's
    country place.

Now who this *Mr. Fox* was
no one seemed to know.
But he was *certainly* brave
and *surely* rich.
And of all her lovers she cared for him alone.

So it was decided
that they should be married.

154

Mr. Fox told her of his castle . . .
told where it was . . .
but strange to say he did not take her to see the place.

So one day when Mr. Fox was away
"on business". . . as he said . . .
Lady Mary set out to see the place where she would
   live.
After some searching she came to the place.
And a fine house it was,
with a moat about it . . . and strong walls.

Lady Mary went to the gate of the castle.
Over the gate was written:
    "BE BOLD, BE BOLD"

    "Well I am *bold*" thought Lady Mary.

So she entered though the gate and went up to
the door of the castle.
Over the door was written:
    "BE BOLD, BE BOLD
    BUT NOT *TOO* BOLD."

    "Well I am *bold* enough," thought Lady Mary.

She opened the door of the castle and went within.
She found no one there,
but broad steps were leading up to a gallery above.
Lady Mary climbed the steps and came to the gallery
   door.
And over the door was written:

"BE BOLD, BE BOLD BUT NOT *TOO* BOLD LEST THAT YOUR HEART'S BLOOD SHOULD RUN *COLD*!"

But that Lady Mary was a *bold* one, she was.
She *opened* the door of that gallery.

And what did she see within?
Why *bodies and bones* of beautiful ladies
all broken and covered with BLOOD!

Lady Mary *ran* from that horrid place.
Back down the stairs . . .
and was about to leave the castle
when she saw through the window . . .
MR. FOX!
coming and dragging another dead lady!

Quickly Lady Mary hid herself behind a cask on the stairs.
And just in time
for Mr. Fox entered the castle and began dragging
the dead body up the stairs behind him
. . . step . . . by step . . . by step . . .
When he came alongside the cask where Lady Mary
   was hiding,
Mr. Fox suddenly spied a ring on the hand of
   the dead lady.
He stopped to try and pull it off.
But it would not come
   so he out with his sword and
hacked off the hand to get the ring!

156

MR. FOX

The hand *flew* into the air and landed of all places . . .
in Lady Mary's *lap*
behind the cask.

Mr. Fox looked about for the hand
  but could not find it.
So he passed on up the stairs
  into the bloody chamber
dragging the dead lady behind him.

As soon as he was gone
Lady Mary ran from the horrid place
  back to her own home.

———

The next morning was the wedding breakfast.
Mr. Fox came to sign the marriage contract.

When all the guests were assembled,
and Mr. Fox seated opposite Lady Mary,
he looked at her

     "How pale you are this morning, my dear," he said.

     "I had bad dreams last night," said Lady Mary.

     "Well, tell us your dreams, my dear.
     And the sound of your sweet voice
     will while away the hour till the time
       of our marriage
     shall come."

"I dreamt,"
said Lady Mary,
"that I went yestermorn to your castle.
And I found there a gate.
And over the gate was written . . .
BE BOLD, BE BOLD."

"Well it *is* not so. And it *was* not so,"
said Mr. Fox.

"I dreamt . . .
that I passed through the gate
  to the door of your castle.
And over the door was written
BE BOLD, BE BOLD.
BUT NOT *TOO* BOLD."

"It *is* not so and it *was* not so,"
said Mr. Fox.

"In my dream . . .
I entered the castle and went up the broad stairs
  to the gallery above.
There I found a door.
Over the door was written
BE BOLD, BE BOLD BUT NOT *TOO* BOLD
LEST THAT YOUR HEART'S BLOOD
SHOULD RUN *COLD*."

"It *is* not so and it *was* not so . . .
'Twas but a dream . . ."
said Mr. Fox.

158

"In my dream. . .
I opened the door of the gallery . . .
And what did I see within??!

Why BODIES AND BONES of Beautiful Ladies
all broken and covered with BLOOD!"

"It IS not so and it WAS not so!
And GOD FORBID that it SHOULD BE so,"
said Mr. Fox.

"Yet in my dream it seems to me . . .
that I ran from that room and started
    down the stairs when I saw
YOU, Mr. Fox,
coming and dragging another dead lady!

I hid behind a cask on the stairs.
You entered the castle and began dragging
    the dead body up the stairs.
When you came alongside the cask where
    I was hiding, you stopped.
And OUT with your sword and
HACKED off her hand to get at the ring!
But the hand flew into the air and landed . . .
of all places . . .
in MY *LAP*!"

"It IS not SO and it WAS not SO and
    HEAVEN FORBID SUCH SHOULD EVER
    be SO!"

cried Mr. Fox
and he started to rise from the table.
"But it IS so and it WAS so!!!
Here's HAND AND RING I have to SHOW!!!"

And so saying Lady Mary leaped from the table . . .
pulled the bloody hand from her dress . . .
and POINTED it at Mr. Fox.

At once her brothers drew their swords
and cut that Mr. Fox
into a thousand pieces!

And thus ends the story
of the *horrid Mr. Fox*
and the *BOLD Lady Mary*.

NOTES ON TELLING

I first heard this tale from Janet Elsner, Pearl City children's librarian in Hawaii. The gory tale is popular with public children's librarians but is so gruesome that most school librarians and teachers dare not tell it. Children, of course, love it. I use the tale in Halloween storytimes. With a little encouragement the group will join in Lady Mary's "Be Bold, Be Bold" as she tells her tale at the wedding breakfast. Make this chant deliberate and ominous.

Strangely, the most gruesome part of the story seems to be the ending, in which Mr. Fox is cut into a thousand pieces. The rest of the tale they find deliciously scary and gory. Obviously, this tale is not for every teller. I see this piece as rolling dramatic action with marvelous language. If you see the tale as horror, perhaps you should not try to tell it. The intent is to delight, not to terrify.

Pacing is everything in this telling. Much of the tale is told very deliberately. But as Lady Mary retells her story, she should become more and more excited until she practically races through the final episode, ending with a gasp on her "It landed . . . in my LAP!"

COMPARATIVE NOTES

My version of this tale follows closely Joseph Jacobs' marvelous rendition in *English Folk and Fairy Tales* (p. 153-158). Jacobs cites his source for the tale as Malone's Variorum Shakespeare (1790). Blakeway contributed the tale to the Variorum to illustrate Benedict's remark in *Much Ado About Nothing*, "Like the old tale, my Lord, It is not so, nor 'twas not so, but indeed, God forbid it should be so." See Jacobs' notes for additional British references to the tale.

Halliwell Phillips includes a version quite similar to the Jacobs version in his 1849 *Popular Rhymes and Nursery Tales* (p. 47-48). He also cites Blakeway's tale as source.

An interesting variant of this tale was collected by T. W. Thompson from Eva Gray (Katharine Briggs, *A Dictionary of British Folk-Tales*, Part A, Vol. II, p. 390). In this variant the tale is told as fact. The girl is asked to come to the home of her suitor Squire King Caley. She finds a brass plate on the door reading "Dr. Foster," a large dog in the kennel, and an old woman in the kitchen who will not speak. A parrot in the parlour warns her to flee. She finds the cellar full of blood and flees as Dr. Foster arrives dragging a captive lady. She hides in the kennel and Dr. Foster throws the lady's hand to the dog. She gets the hand from the dog and reaches home. Her father sets a trap for King Caley by inviting him to a storytelling party. Scotland Yard detectives come disguised as farmers and the girl is disguised as a young man. All tell their dreams. When her turn comes she tells the tale and produces the hand. It is recognized as belonging to the fiancée of one of the guests. King Caley is arrested and hanged.

This tale is Type 955 *The Robber Bridegroom*. Aarne-Thompson's tale type index lists sources from Germany, Finland, Sweden, Estonia, Livonia, Lithuania, Denmark, Iceland, Ireland, England, France, the Netherlands, Austria, Rumania, Hungary, Czechoslovakia, Russia, and Greece as well as Lappish, Serbocroatian, and Franco-American variants. In addition, Thompson lists a variant from India under his motif K1916 *Robber bridegroom. Robber marries girl under picture of being a fine gentleman.*

MacDonald indexes this tale as S62.1 *Bluebeard. Girl marries murderous husband.* In Perrault's "Bluebeard" a bride opens a forbidden door and finds corpses and blood. She drops a key in the blood and is found out. She asks respite to say prayers and stalls until her brothers come and kill Bluebeard. In the Grimm's tale "Robber Bridegroom" a bride visits her bridegroom's house, strewing peas to find her way home. An old woman hides her and the hand of the victim falls near her. She produces this hand at the wedding feast and tells her tale. See *The Classic Fairy Tales* by Iona and Peter Opie for further discussion of this tale.

These tales are also related to Type 311 *Rescue by the sister (who deceives the ogre into carrying the girls in a sack [chest] back to their home).* This tale often contains the motif of a forbidden chamber in which the girl drops an egg, key, apple, etc. soiling it.

MacDonald lists several variants of this tale under Motif G561.1 *Girls in ogre's power not to enter forbidden chamber.* The Grimm tale "Fitcher's Feathered Bird" is an example of this tale.

PUNIA AND THE KING OF THE SHARKS

Once in the Bay of Kohala
on the Big Island of Hawaii
there lived a boy whose name was Punia.*

Punia lived with his mother
for his father had been killed by Kai-ale-ale,**
the King of the Sharks.

---

*Pronounced Poo-née-ä
**Pronounced Käee-älee-älcc

In the Bay of Kohala there lived
TEN BIG SHARKS.
Kai-ale-ale was the KING of all the sharks.

No one could dive into the bay
for squid, or fish, or lobster to eat
because of the *sharks*.

The people of Kohala had only sweet potatoes and
    vegetables to eat.
They did not dare dive for seafood.

One day Punia's mother said:
      "If only I had a bite of lobster to go with
         my sweet potato.
         Everyday it is sweet potato . . . sweet potato . . .
         sweet potato . . ."

Punia said:
      "Mother, I will get you some lobster."

Punia went to the Bay of Kohala.
He looked down into the water.
There were the ten sharks
swimming with King Kai-ale-ale.

Punia lifted a large rock . . .
he called:
      "It is *I*, the Boy *Punia*.

164

I have come to dive into the Bay of Kohala
and bring up a lobster for my mother's dinner."

Then he threw the rock into the water.

At once King Kai-ale-ale and his ten sharks
swam to where the rock had fallen.
They meant to tear Punia to bits.
But they found only a rock.

Punia had dived *behind* the sharks.
He went into the cave,
took a lobster in each hand
and swam back to the shore.

Then he called to the sharks:
    "King Kai-ale-ale . . . I have TRICKED you!
    It was one of your *own* sharks
    who told me what to do.
    It was the first shark . . . the second shark . . .
      the third shark . . .
    the fourth shark . . . the fifth shark . . .
      the sixth shark . . .
    the seventh shark . . . the eighth shark . . .
      the ninth shark . . .
    the tenth shark . . . It was the TENTH shark.
      The one with
    the *thin* tail who told me what to do!"

At that all of the sharks turned

and chased the TENTH shark away from the
   Bay of Kohala.

The next day the Boy Punia went to the Bay again.
He called:
   "It is *I*, the Boy *Punia*.
   I have come to dive into the water
   and bring up a lobster for my mother's dinner."

Then he threw a stone into the Bay.

At once the sharks *raced* to where the stone
   had fallen
and tried to tear it to shreds.

But Punia dived behind them,
went into the cave,
took a lobster in each hand
and swam back to the shore.

   "King Kai-ale-ale . . . I have TRICKED you
      again.
   It was the first shark . . . the second shark . . . the
   third shark . . . the fourth shark . . . the fifth
      shark . . .
   the sixth shark . . . the seventh shark . . . the
      eighth
   shark . . . the ninth shark . . . It was the NINTH
      shark!
   The one with the *bent nose* . . . who told me what
   to do!"

166

The sharks TURNED on that NINTH shark.
And drove him away from the Bay of Kohala.

The next day Punia went again to the Bay of Kohala.
He tricked the sharks AGAIN.

> "King Kai-ale-ale . . .
> It was the first shark . . . the second shark . . .
>   the third shark . . .
> the fourth shark . . . the fifth shark . . .
>   the sixth shark . . .
> the seventh shark . . . the eighth shark . . .
>   It was the EIGHTH shark!
> The one with the *big stomach* . . .
>   who told me what to do!"

And they chased THAT shark away.

Punia did this until *all the sharks were gone* except one.
And that one was
KING KAI-ALE-ALE.

Punia took his bag of sticks
and went to the Bay of Kohala.
He called loudly:
>   "I must dive into the water one more time
>   to get a lobster for my mother's dinner.
>   If King Kai-ale-ale *bites* me,
>   my blood will come to the surface of the water

167

and my mother will see it
and bring me back to *life*.
But if King Kai-ale-ale takes me into his mouth
   WHOLE
I will die forever."

King Kai-ale-ale thought:
   "I will not bite that Boy.
   I will not let his blood go to the top of the water.
   I will take him into my mouth *whole*."

And he took Punia into his mouth
without biting him.

As soon as he was inside King Kai-ale-ale's mouth
Punia took out his bag of sticks.
He propped two large sticks . . .
"FOM! FOM!"
right between King Kai-ale-ale's jaws.
Now King Kai-ale-ale could not *close* his mouth.

Punia took from his bag his *fire* sticks
and began to build a fire
on the *tongue* of King Kai-ale-ale.

It became HOT!
HOT! . . .
HOTTER! . . .
King Kai-ale-ale *rushed* from the Bay
he thrashed about the ocean
groaning. . . .

168

He swam *back* to the Bay of Kohala
with Punia still in his mouth.

Punia saw that they were nearing the Bay of Kohala.
He heard the waves breaking on the reef, and he
thought:
>"If King Kai-ale-ale takes me near the reef,
>where the waves break on the rocks,
>I will surely *die*.
>But if he takes me to the sandy shore,
>where the grasses grow,
>I will *live*."

So Punia called:
>"I am in great *danger*.
>If King Kai-ale-ale takes me to the reef
>where the breakers crash,
>I am SAVED!
>But if he takes me to the sandy shore
>where the grasses grow,
>I will DIE."

When King Kai-ale-ale heard this he thought
>"I will not take that boy Punia to the reef
>where the breakers crash.
>I will take him to the sandy shore
>where the grasses grow.
>And he shall DIE."

King Kai-ale-ale swam with the Boy Punia far up
into the sandy shallows.

He swam where no shark had ever gone before.

And when he reached the sandy shore
where the grasses grow . . .
King Kai-ale-ale got *stuck* in the sand.
He could not return to the deep waters.

Then Punia jumped from the shark's mouth
and called all the people of Kohala.
They brought their spears and knives
and killed the giant shark.

From then on
the people of Kohala
could dive again in their own Bay of Kohala,
thanks to the Boy Punia.

NOTES ON TELLING

The two episodes in this tale make it feel like two tales. This may be a difficult tale for the beginning storyteller, so don't try it as one of your first efforts. The sharks, however, never fail to excite audiences and this theme assures you of eager listeners.

The counting out bit in the tale can be used to involve the audience. Point to individuals in the audience as you count the sharks . . . it was the first . . . the second . . . the third . . . the one with the thin fin! The audience may join you in the counting. You may contract or expand this counting out routine depending on your audience. If it starts to get tedious, just cut to the last shark. With pre-schoolers I sometimes chant, "It was the first . . . the second . . . the third . . . the one with the blond hair" (or green dress . . . etc.). The personalization delights them.

When Karen Bawden, a very dramatic teller, performs this tale she "throws" the rock far to the right, then "dives" to the left. She reverses this each time to continue tricking the sharks. Karen "swims" under water, holding her breath and breaststroking to grab her lobsters and swim back to the top. Such dramatizations, while not for everyone, work well for some tellers. When Punia taunts the shark king, Karen includes a chant from Vivian Laubach Thompson's *Hawaiian Legends of Tricksters and Riddlers* (p. 24).

"Mahalo King of the Restless Sea!
Thank you for giving these LOBSTERS to me!"

Karen's Punia lives in the stomach of King Kai-ale-ale for three days, scraping fat from the shark's insides to eat.

COMPARATIVE NOTES:

Padraic Colum includes "Punia and the King of the Sharks" in *Legends of Hawaii*. He cites as his source the Fornander Collection of Hawaiian Antiquities and Folklore, Memoirs of the Bernice Pauahi Bishop Museum, v.V, Part II. Tale "Kaao no Punia."

Martha Beckwith includes the tale in her *Hawaiian Mythology*. She also cites Fornander as a source but gives a more extended tale than Colum. In the Fornander version as given by Beckwith, Punia lives for ten days inside the shark, eating the shark's flesh to stay alive. Weakened, the shark finally heads for shore. The story then continues with a final episode:

"On his way back to Kohala, Punia escapes the spirits by pretending that this fishing ground is familiar to him and thus enticing the spirits out to sea by ones and twos where they are at his mercy. Thus he kills all but one wary spirit."

Beckwith, p. 43.

The marvelous counting out device . . ."It was the first . . . the second . . . the third . . ." may have been added by Colum as a storytelling device. Beckwith's version does not include it.

Beckwith also describes a parallel tale from Samoa in which Alele spirits steal the yams of the Tui Samata, who sends his grandson La-le-a-sapai to recover them. The boy throws a club into their bathing pool and the spirits fight each other until all are killed.

Thompson classifies the tale as K341.16 *Stone thrown to attract attention of shark guardians. Man then slips in cave and steals lobsters.* He cites only Beckwith. MacDonald cites Padraic Colum (*Legends of Hawaii,* and *Stone of Victory*), Vivian Laubach Thompson (*Hawaiian Legends of Tricksters and Riddlers*), and a picture book version by Beverly Mohan (*Punia and the King of the Sharks*). All of these versions seem to have been taken from the Fornander tale. Bacil F. Kirtley's *Motif-Index of Traditional Polynesian Narratives* lists only Beckwith and Fornander.

The first part of this tale is Motif K1080 *Persons duped into injuring each other.* This is a fairly widespread motif, though not in the form taken by the Punia tale. The dupes may be brought to fight by such stratagems as striking one and making him think the other hit him (K1082), throwing a missile among the dupes (K1082.1), or by lying to the dupes (K1084). See Thompson and MacDonald for numerous variants.

The second part of the tale is Motif F912 *Victim kills swallower from within* and Motif F811.4 *Jonah. Fish or water monster swallows a man.* This is another widespread motif, with many African, Native American, and Polynesian variants. Beckwith cites five variants of a tale about a hero called Kae who is swallowed by a whale, shark, or large fish and kills it from within (p. 502-504).

Interesting Polynesian variants of this motif include a Roratongan tale of a girl swallowed by a fish (James Holding, *The Sky-Eater*, p. 75-86). She cuts slits in the fish's throat and escapes — hence, fish have gills. Beckwith includes the tale of a little shark hero who kills a giant shark by swimming into his mouth and devouring his insides (p. 138).

Kirtley lists 24 Polynesian variants of F912 *Victim kills swallower from within*. In nine of Kirtley's variants the victim emerges bald. One of Beckwith's Kae variants shows Kae emerging bald from the stomach of the whale.

Several Native American tales are reminiscent of the Punia tale. In a Cherokee variant, a hunter is swallowed by a giant fish. He cuts his way out with a mussel shell. His head is bald from the stomach acids (Dee Brown, *Tepee Tales of the American Indian*, p. 132-33). Other Native American variants include a Chippewa tale in which Manabozho kills a giant sturgeon from within by cutting out its heart (Thomas Leekley, *The World of Manabozho*, p.79-91), and a Haida tale in which Kagwaii, the giant whale, eats a boy disguised as a halibut (Christie Harris, *Once Upon a Totem*, p. 33-58). An Eskimo tale shows Raven killing a whale by drinking whale oil inside the whale (Gail Robinson and Douglas Hill, *Coyote the Trickster*, p. 85-94).

For more swallowed heroes see MacDonald F911 through F915.

THE MAGIC FOX

In Japan there are *magic foxes*.
These foxes can change themselves into anything they
   wish: . . . a wooodcutter . . . a crying baby . . . a tree . . .
   or a leaf . . .
They are *very* tricky.

Once in Japan
there lived a boy
whose name was Zuiten.

Zuiten lived in a Buddhist temple
high in the mountains.

Zuiten's job was to sweep the temple every day,
dust the altar where the golden statue of the
   Lord Buddha sat
and cook the rice for the evening meal.

One day when Zuiten was in the kitchen preparing the
   rice pot,
he thought he heard someone call his name.

   "Zui . . . ten . . . Zui . . . ten . . ."

174

THE MAGIC FOX

Zuiten went into the temple and slid back the
 shoji* door . . .
he looked out . . .

But there was no one there.

Zuiten went back to the kitchen and began
 washing his rice.
 "Zui . . . ten . . . Zui . . . ten . . ."

Zuiten ran to the door.
He *slid* the shoji aside . . .
There was no one there.

Zuiten thought:
 "There is something *strange* here.
 I will just wait and see what is going on."

Zuiten hid beside the door and waited.

Now the shoji doors of the temple
were made of rice paper and wooden slats.
They would slide aside as you opened them.

In the forest near the temple
lived a *magic fox*.
This tricky fox would sneak out of the forest
and creep up to the temple door.

---

*Pronounced shō-jee

With his bushy tail
he would *brush* across the wooden slats of the
   shoji door
making a noise like . . .
     "Zui . . .
     Zui . . .
     Zui . . ."

With his head
he would *knock* on the rice paper panes of
   the door
making a sound like . . .
     "ten . . .
     ten . . .
     ten . . ."

This sounded as if he were calling:
     "Zui . . . ten . . .
     Zui . . . ten . . .
     Zui . . . ten. . ."

Zuiten hid beside the door.
The *next* time that fox brushed "Zui . . . zui . . . zui . . ."
Zuiten got ready.

When the fox knocked "Ten . . . ten . . . ten . . ."
Zuiten *slid* back the door!
The magic fox tumbled head first into the temple.
Zuiten closed the shoji door.
He had *caught* the magic fox.

176

THE MAGIC FOX

The magic fox *jumped* to his feet.
He began to *race* around the temple.
Faster . . . and faster . . . and FASTER . . .
until . . . POOF!!!
He was *gone*.

Zuiten *looked* around the temple room.
That fox had turned himself into *something* . . .
What could he be?
Then Zuiten saw it.
On the altar where sat the golden statue of the
   Lord Buddha . . .
there were now *two* Buddhas!
Which was the *real* Lord Buddha . . . ?
And which was the *fox* Buddha . . . ?

Zuiten was clever.
He went to the altar and bowed.

> "I'll soon know which is the *real* Buddha,"
>   he said.
> "Whenever I say my prayers . . .
> the *real* Buddha always
> STICKS OUT HIS TONGUE."

Now of course the *real* Buddha
would never stick out his tongue.
But the fox didn't know that.

Zuiten began to say his prayers.
Slowly he began to beat the temple drum.

"Poku . . . Poku . . . Poku . . ."
And slowly . . .
the Buddha on the *left* . . .
stuck out his TONGUE!

"Mmmhmmm . . . I see . . ." said Zuiten.
"After I say my prayers
the *real* Buddha always
follows me down the hall to the kitchen."

Zuiten turned and walked slowly down the hall
   to the kitchen.
And slowly . . .
the *fox* Buddha
climbed down from the altar and
      "TOKU . . . TOKU . . . TOKU . . ."
he followed Zuiten down the hall.

"Mmmhmmm . . . I see . . ." said Zuiten.
"Now after prayers
the *real* Buddha always
has a *bath* in the *rice pot*."

Zuiten lifted the big wooden lid
and slowly . . .
the *fox* Buddha *climbed* into the rice pot.

Zuiten popped on the lid
and began building up the *fire* under the rice pot.

Suddenly

"Whirrrrrrrr . . .
POP . . . POP. . . POP. . . POP"
Out popped four fox legs.
Out popped a fox *tail* . . . !

Zuiten lifted the lid
OUT jumped the magic fox.
Off he ran
"TONPIKANKO!"
over the hill and into the forest.

The fox never came back to bother Zuiten again.

NOTES ON TELLING

I include "Zuiten" because it is such a delightful tale, and because it is available in only one children's collection, and that unfortunately is out-of-print (Elizabeth Scofield, *A Fox in One Bite*, Kodansha, 1965, 33-39).

I do not usually tell this as an audience participation tale, although when telling to pre-schoolers I do sometimes involve them in a bit of body language play on the fox's "Zui . . . ten" at the story's beginning.

When telling the tale be sure to accord the statue of the Lord Buddha the same respect that you would give to a statue of the deity in a Christian tale.

COMPARATIVE NOTES

Stories of magic foxes and magic badgers are legion in Japan. American children are familiar with them mostly through the Japanese story of the dancing teakettle (MacDonald D1161.3.1). MacDonald's *Storyteller's Sourcebook* alone cites 12 children's sources for this tale, indication of its popularity in the United States. In the dancing teakettle story a fox or badger disguised as a teakettle is brought into the temple. Once inside it turns back to its real form and the young acolytes attempt to catch it. The similarity between the dancing teakettle tales and our story ends there, as our tale proceeds with a series of trick-the-fox motifs.

The trickery in this tale is related to Motif K710+ *Victim enticed into voluntary captivity or helplessness* and K607 *Enemy in ambush (or disguise) deceived into declaring himself.* MacDonald lists many African and Asian variants of such trickster-tricked motifs.

The most useful version of this tale appears in Elizabeth Scofield's *A Fox in One Bite.* Scofield prepared her collection, which includes six tales of magic foxes, while teaching at an international primary school in Tokyo. MacDonald classifies this tale as K607.4* and gives also a related tale in which a witch turns into a statue of the goddess Kannon. A man tricks her by saying that the statue of Kannon always smiles and reaches for food when offered. He throws the witch/Kannon into a boiling pot (Garret Bang, *Men from the Village Deep in the Mountains,* p. 61-65).

These tales seem to be of great antiquity. M. W. DeVissen ("The Fox and Badger in Japanese Folklore," *Transactions of the Asiatic Society of Japan,* XXXVI, Part 3, 1908, p. 39) relates a tale in which a tanuki badger appears in the form of a Bodhisattva seated on a white elephant. In this case the badger appears as the living god rather than his statue.

MacDonald lists other badger/fox stories under D612.1 *Illusory transformation of animals in order to sell and cheat*; D421.8 *Transformation: badger to object*; and D313.1.1 *Transformation: fox to person.* An especially popular children's badger story is Claus Stamm's *The Very Special Badgers* (Viking, 1960). In this picture book the badgers are called "Cheat-and-change" badgers, since they change their form in order to cheat.

See Richard Dorson's *Folk Legends of Japan* (p. 128) for further discussion and bibliography on the fox legend in Japan.

PART II: NOTES

FINDING, LEARNING, AND
TELLING TALES

This chapter will offer suggestions for learning and telling stories. Let's begin with the understanding that *storytelling is a folk art*; a form of expression that belongs to all of us. Your contribution to a tale will be your special telling of it. Play with your material and make it your own. Develop a style you find comfortable, and a repertoire tailored to your particular folk audience. *You and your class of children form a folk group*, and each time you share a new tale, you make it uniquely yours.

Now, with this in mind, let's turn for a moment to the storytelling event. Storytelling is distinct from conversational speech, because through body language, delivery, and attitude, the teller enters a performing mode. And yet, this performance is distinct too from traditional theatrical performance; it is more intimate, and a sense of comradery develops between teller and audience. *Storytelling is an audience shaped art form*. It is more than just performance, it is an event involving both audience and teller in a constant interplay of tension. Interaction may become vocal, approaching group drama, or it may be merely an emotional intensity, but the interplay between audience and teller is the heart of the storytelling event. Be receptive to your audiences' responses; learn to trust their aesthetic sense. Remember, no tale is ever finished. *Tales are by their nature works in progress.*

From the storytelling event then, let's move to the tales themselves. Let's begin with the realization that *there is no one final tale text*. There are only transcriptions of tales taken from single tellings by individual storytellers. Keep in mind that each tale changes from telling to telling and from teller to teller, and so there will be infinite variants of every text. An important factor that will determine the meaning a tale takes on is the context in which it is told. *Each storytelling event functions within its own cultural context.* Your telling will function quite uniquely within an American cultural context defined by your setting.

So, now let's grant ourselves a few permissions as storytellers. First of all, *we may practice the art of storytelling even if we are not master tellers.* Ideally, every tale should be perfected before we offer it to an audience. But in our busy lives this requirement merely inhibits our use of storytelling. Let's give ourselves permission to begin telling a tale before it is perfect. Plunge on in and let the audience help mold the story. Keep telling and telling until the tale becomes perfect. Secondly, *it is all right to tell the tales of cultures other than our own.* We should find out as much as possible about the functions of these tales in their own societies, learn about the context in which the tale was originally told, and share this information with our audiences. But, we need not feel compelled to tell a story with a high degree of ethnic authenticity. It is unlikely that we will be able to do this anyway unless we have roots in the contributing culture. We must realize that in our telling, a tale will change and reflect the new context in which it is told. Tales have been passing from culture to culture for centuries. When we borrow a tale from another culture, we enjoy it, appreciate it, and through our telling, make it distinctly ours. Let's give ourselves permission to relax and tell stories our way. You, your tale, and your audience create a unique event. You are not replicating, you are creating. Feel free to enjoy yourself!

FINDING THE TALE

Finding the tale is perhaps your hardest task. Once you have discovered a tale that excites you, the rest is easy. To help you compile your own personal list of tellable tales, I've suggested four tactics.

First, browse through collections of folktales and short stories. This is a time-consuming endeavor, and you may scan dozens of collections before discovering one tale you want to learn. With time you will become skilled in recognizing at a glance tales that you can make your own.

Second, mine specific areas. You will discover that certain ethnic areas, or certain tale genres will particularly delight you. Once you have identified these favorite areas, order all the books available and search them for tales you might learn.

Third, keep lists. As you browse, note those tales that you might want to learn some day. Go over your lists every few months to see if one of those tales excites you now. Sometimes a good tale will lie dormant in your imagination for years and then suddenly leap out from the lists ready to be learned and told.

Finally, borrow from other tellers. Storytelling is an oral art form, passed more easily from teller to teller than from teller-to-collector-to-author-to-book-to-teller. A tale that seems dead on the printed page can suddenly leap to life, the possibilities for telling made obvious, when we hear it performed by another teller. Most tellers are glad to have their tales passed on by other tellers. Traditional tales often end with an admonition to the listener to do just that.

Once you have selected your tale it is wise to shop around for the best possible variant. Check available folklore references such as MacDonald's *Storyteller's Sourcebook* to see if other variants of that tale are available. Compare variants to choose the best version for your telling. You may even want to combine motifs from several variants for your own tale.

I suggest that you start with short tales with repetitive elements. Chants, onomatopoeic words, songs, and catchy phrases all act as mnemonic devices for the teller. The language of the tale is also important. Look for tales couched in direct language, which cuts straight to the heart of the matter. The language should possess a rhythm and cadence that allows it to read aloud well. Avoid tales that are overly flowery or burdened with descriptive passages. The more difficult literary redactions of tales require memorization for success. Unless you memorize with ease, leave those beautifully worded literary masterpieces for the more experienced teller.

And of course, choose only tales that delight you. A tale must be so good that you can't wait to tell it to someone!

Preparing a Tale Text from a Children's Short Story

Few of our children's folktale collections contain tales that
can be immediately told. Most have been rewritten into the
short story format, removing the tale from its original oral telling. You may need to unwrite a tale before you can tell it.
There are, however, two exceptions to this. Literary variants,
such as those by Pyle and Anderson, chosen for their fine language, should be committed to memory and reproduced in
their original text. Also, there are a few folktale collections
available in which the printed versions of the tales remain close
to the oral tellings. A bibliography of such collections is included in this book in the section entitled *Sources*. The beginning teller might start by selecting tales from that bibliography. If, however, you find yourself with a tale in an unwieldy
short story form that you'd like to tell, you may find the following suggestions for reshaping a tale helpful.

> Read the story through several times to become familiar
> with the flow of the storyline. You should have a feel
> for the sweep of the tale from beginning to end, the con-
> stant forward movement of plot, and the overall form
> of the tale.
>
> As you go through, mark any especially well-turned
> phrases, magical words, or chants that you want to re-
> tain in your own telling.
>
> Does your tale include repetition? If so, make sure that
> your final version gives the repetition its rightful place.
> Keep the repeated elements parallel in their form, or
> nearly so. The aesthetics of the folktale demand this.
>
> Examine the beginning and ending of the tale. Do you
> want to retain the author's phrasing, or could the open-
> ing and closing be reworded for better effect? The be-
> ginning and ending must be perfect.
>
> Read the entire tale aloud. If any phrases are too long,
> too wordy, or too much of a side-track from the tale's

progress, mark them out. Descriptive phrases, if used at all, should be simple and pertinent; extensive dialog should be cut. Each word must be necessary. Master tellers skilled at holding an audience can reverse this process and spin out a tale with lengthy elaborations, but the beginning teller should strive for simplicity and directness in telling. At every step of your tale, ask yourself these questions: Is it necessary? Is it beautiful? Is it fun? If a sentence fulfills none of these functions, consider cutting it.

Read through your edited version aloud. Does it flow? Does the sound of it please you? Have you cut too much and lost some of the flavor of the piece?

Continue reworking until you have a version that reads aloud well and communicates the essence of your tale.

LEARNING THE TALE

A tale can be prepared for a first telling without hours of practice. A five-minute tale can usually be learned in about an hour and a half. It will not, however, be perfect. Not yet. As soon as you know the tale, you must begin telling it. Let your audiences work on the tale through their responses. You will shape and refine the tale through repeated tellings.

By choosing just the right tale for your own telling style and your audience, you will already have done the hardest part. In your first hour of practice you must find a spot where you cannot be disturbed. You must be able to pace about, gesture, rant and rave as the tale dictates. Many tellers feel that they learn best when working on their feet, moving with the tale and throwing their entire body into the learning effort. Later tellings may be more restrained, but this method often helps in the early stages. Here are some suggested steps for easy learning.

Read your tale through.

Read the tale again, this time out loud. Listen to the

sound of the language. Watch for pacing, cadences, the flow of the language.

Read it out loud again. This time, stop to memorize the beginning and the ending and any chants or key phrases. The first sentence must be absolutely perfect, a magical entré into the land of the imagination. Committing the final phrase to memory assures you a polished, confident flourish at the tale's end.

Now, put down the book and begin to tell the tale in your own words. The rest of the tale should not be memorized. If your language seems stiff or hesitant, go back to the text to see how that author handled the tale. Use the text as a hint, not a frozen fact. Tell the tale as far as you can remember, then stop and check your progress with the text. Note any changes you want to make in your telling and begin again. Continue until you have gotten through the entire tale.

Tell the whole tale out loud one more time.

If you have concentrated well, this one hour of hard work should fix the tale in your mind. Each teller will develop a unique learning style. Some tellers learn by making mental pictures of the tale's scenes and "seeing" these as they tell. Others rely on the flow of the language and take their cues from the sound and rhythm of the prose. Whatever mnemonic devices you use, it is important that you have a clear sense of the sequence of events within the tale.

Between your first, hour-long learning session and your second rehearsal, you should tell the tale to yourself two or three times. Check back with the text if important phrases or events have escaped you. Use odd moments of time to work on your story. Tell it aloud while driving to work, tell it silently while waiting for the doctor. Sing it in the shower.

Final Tale Rehearsal: ½ Hour

On the day of your first performance, plan for another half hour of complete concentration to rehearse your tale. Again find a place where you can pace about and talk out loud.

> First, tell the tale out loud. Imagine the audience to whom you will be telling. Face them and tell to them. Imagine yourself communicating with them as you tell. (Later, when you are more confident, add a telling before a mirror at this rehearsal. At this early stage in your career, however, the naked truth might scare you so much you would never go on stage. So save that excellent polishing technique for later in your storytelling career.)
>
> Take time to smooth out any problems in your telling. Practice a difficult phrase or two.
>
> Perform the polished tale for your imaginary audience one last time.
>
> Tell yourself that you are fantastic! You are ready for your audience!

TALE PERFORMANCE

It's time. Your moment has arrived. Here are a few suggestions to help you through your first telling.

> Pause before you launch into your tale. Gather your audience together with your silence. Let your body language and your manner tell them that something extraordinary is about to begin.
>
> Take special care with your opening phrase. This is the magical moment, the bridge between the ordinary

and the fabulous. Make certain that the crossing is deliberate.

Throughout the telling be aware of your audience. Speak *to* them. You are telling them something important. Maintain eye contact and try to be aware of each person's response to your story. As you master your storytelling skills this will become easier. The better you know your tale, the easier it will be for you to relax and experience your audience as you tell.

Keep close rein on the pacing of your tale. It will need to be just right to produce the effect you want. Experimentation with many audiences will help you find the right pace: when to pause, when to go slow, when to race ahead, when to pounce!

Be sure to do justice to the beauty of language in your tale. Take your time with any especially lovely phrases, poetic chants, or extraordinary words. Let your audience feel from your handling that you love speaking these phrases just as much as they are going to love hearing them.

Your body language and your manner should show your self-confidence and control throughout the telling. You are on stage. This is performance. Hide your quaking knees and stride into your story with assurance. This is your moment and you are responsible for holding your audience aloft throughout the telling.

The ending, as the beginning, must be deliberate and perfect. Let the audience down gently, then stand quietly for a moment as the group returns to reality.

Accept your kudos and give yourself a pat on the back. You've earned it! Should your audience not respond with reinforcing vocal approval at the end of your telling, do not take this as a sign of failure. Some audiences clap, some exclaim, some sit quietly and think.

AFTER THE TELLING

Find another audience as soon as possible and tell the tale again. Tell the tale as often as you can in the next few weeks. After each telling take a few moments to consider ways in which this telling was better or worse than previous tellings. Once the tale has assumed a comfortable form, tape record a performance. Keep this for future reference. Ten years from now you will be able to easily prepare this tale again for performance by listening to your own perfected telling.

Repeated Performance As a Tale Polishing Technique

The key to my method of minimum rehearsal tale learning is repeated performance. The teller must engineer situations in which the same tale can be told several times within a short period of time. The school librarian will find this easy; simply tell your new story to every class that visits your library this week. Once you get your confidence up, you will find that even the dreaded sixth grade will be looking forward to your tales! The classroom teacher must work a bit harder to find repeated telling opportunities. The other second grade teacher might be glad to trade classes and let you tell stories to her class. Perhaps you could pop into the kindergarten at lunch break long enough to tell a quick story. Don't forget that your own students will love hearing the same tale repeated. If it strikes their imaginations, they may want to hear it several times!

As a public librarian, I plan repetitive storytelling opportunities into my yearly schedule. Each spring I visit the 12 schools in my library service area, telling a story in each class as I talk about our summer reading program. That gives me a chance to tell well over 200 times. In October I invite Scouts, Campfires, and neighborhood groups to visit the library for private Halloween storytimes. I tell my set of Halloween stories over 20 times in the two weeks preceding Halloween. Storytelling program exchanges with other libraries enable each librarian to tell her stories at several libraries in the county, while other tellers visit her library.

To perfect a new tale, you must set up such repeated storytelling experiences for yourself. A single tale telling will not leave you with a polished tale, no matter how hard you work.

USING AUDIENCE PARTICIPATION

The tales I have chosen for this collection all have audience participation possibilities. Skillful use of audience participation requires considerable experience, and this may seem an unusual technique to suggest for the beginning storyteller. The immediate reinforcement that the teller receives from a group involved in an audience participation story is rewarding, however, to even the most inexperienced teller. These tales will all work quite well without audience participation, so you must choose the telling style that suits you best. Here are some hints for those who wish to try these tales using audience participation.

Chose stories that are repetive; full of refrains, chants, and songs, because these immediately invite audience participation. Once the members of your audience have warmed up to you as a teller, they will need only a glance of encouragement from you to join in vocally.

To get the audience to join in on a refrain, pause, gather the group with your eyes, and let them know by an air of expectation that you want them to help you with whatever comes next. Nod encouragement to those who do chime in and soon the whole group will be participating. It usually is not necessary to ask the group verbally "Do you want to help me say the chant?" Sometimes a new audience needs this encouragement at first.

It is important to keep cueing your audience deftly so they always know just what is expected of them. If you intend to use audience participation as a part of your tale, make your cueing a part of your tale rehearsal. You must lead them, not wait to see how they will respond. A simple hand gesture, slight nod of the head, or glance can cue the audience to respond or to return to silence.

If a group does not join in, be adaptable. Change your style and tell the story without the participatory approaches. Some groups are more comfortable listening quietly.

ORIGINS OF THE FOLKTALE TEXT

Many folktales published for children were first told orally as audience participation tales. Some even included singing and dancing in their performances. Unfortunately, few collections include the kind of information that will help us reproduce the tales as they were originally told.

How are these delightful oral traditions lost in the process of becoming children's books? Consider the way in which children's folktale collections are prepared.

The collection is most often put together by a professional writer. The would-be folktale author goes first to a research library and examines tale collections there in the hope of finding some tales that might make good children's material. Finding a few, he brings them home and rewrites them in a short story format that he thinks will appeal to children. He may simplify vocabulary and add lots of conversation if he is trying to market this for the younger reader. He may add descriptive passages and ethnic details to give the story more character. A single page text from a folktale journal may easily expand to several pages before it reaches print.

And what of the text from which the writer was working? Before the days of the tape recorder, this text was probably taken down by hand. It is likely that the tale was told by an informant reiterating cultural information for a researching anthropologist, but only rarely will these tales have been taken down from a teller in actual performance.

There are problems with this method of tale collecting. In every culture we find both active and passive bearers of story-telling traditions. Probably every person in the United States could tell the story of Cinderella to a researcher, if questioned. Few would, however, stand up before a group and offer to tell this tale as entertainment. We are all passive bearers of much folktale material. We know the tales, but we don't pass them on. Only a few individuals assume the role of "storyteller" and become active bearers of folktale traditions. Obviously the tale text collected from a passive bearer will be quite unlike the rendition possible from an active bearer. The tales recorded

192

in anthropological journals were not always taken down from the group's master storytellers, so the texts may be less than perfect to begin with. Even if a master teller was located for research, it was seldom arranged that his tale be taken down during an actual performance, and thus, the tale as given will lack the excitement generated by a live audience.

Because of the way in which these tale texts were taken down, and because researchers, until recently, showed little interest in tale performance itself, the printed texts seldom include information about the tale telling event. If parts of the tale were sung or danced, this is rarely noted. If the audience participated in the telling, we are not told this. Sometimes chants or words for songs within the tale text are included, but musical notation is not given. The bare bones tale texts from which many of our children's collections have been prepared are sadly lacking in tale performance information.

A brief bibliography of collections which do not remove their tales far from the performance mode is given on page 202. Of these, the most noteworthy is Diane Wolkstein's *The Magic Orange Tree*. Diane, a New York City storyteller of considerable renown, went to Haiti to collect stories. She has recorded these tales in performance, and she describes each performance in a brief note accompanying her tales. She tells us how the performer moved, how the audience responded. Her tales are translated into English with the audience in mind, and can be taken from the printed page and sprung back into a performing mode with ease.

Unfortunately, Diane Wolkstein's book is quite unique. The folklorist's interest in performance style and contextual information about storytelling events seems to have made no impact on the children's publishing industry. Authors continue to research from antiquated journals and rewrite folktales as short stories. Even travelers who have lived abroad and heard stories told in their true settings revert to a short story format when retelling for children's publications. They seldom include performance or contextual information. Ideally, a children's folktale collection should meet the following criteria:

The tale should be collected from a master teller in a telling context usual to the community.

The tale should be translated by an individual skilled in the nuances of both English and the tale's native language. Translation is an art and requires a high degree of literary skill. Folktale translations should remain as close to the master teller's recorded text as is possible. The translator should attempt to show also the contextual flavor of the tale. Audience reactions may be important components of the storytelling event. Songs and chants within the story should be transcribed and included in the text with musical notations. A collection might even contain an accompanying record with a musical rendition of the songs included or a recording of the actual tale telling event.

The collection author should include information about the tale teller, the community from which the tale was collected, and the storytelling event itself. A discussion of the tale's function in this society and cultural information about the group using the tale can be included.

A scholarly note for each tale should be included giving the tale's motif and type numbers and discussing other variants of the tale briefly.

If we who use children's folktale collections know what we want, perhaps we can convince publishers to produce more useful tale collections.

STORYTELLING STYLES

Beginning tellers often worry about achieving an "authentic" storytelling style. A look at folk tellings throughout the world soon shows us that there are many different telling styles. Some cultures dictate a particular style of telling, but what is aesthetically pleasing in one culture may be considered poor storytelling by another culture. In any case, there almost always seems to be a place for the innovative artist who breaks with all tradition and tells in his or her own inimitable manner.

Within our own culture we can observe the public library tradition of storytelling. For years the storytellers in public library children's rooms have favored a restrained style of delivery. Beginning librarians have been taught carefully the art of speaking with well-modulated voice, while keeping hands and body still. This restrained delivery style has proved effective for many tellers.

A preference for a restrained telling style can also be found in folk tradition. Roger Abrahams, in his discussion of the ballad singer Alameda Riddle, expressed this philosophy well: "She insists that a good traditional singer must *present* and not *perform* the songs. By this she means that the song must come first, that the singer must not throw himself into the singing."[1]

MacEdward Leach portrays a similar style in his discussion of ballad singer John Snead. "He'd sit in the chair, head back and eyes closed as he sang. Like all folksingers he let the song speak: it was all dead-pan—no histrionics, no acting. The story came through uninterrupted by singer or background accompaniment. Ballad understatement, ballad simplicity, and ballad starkness could build up their effect unobstructed."[2]

Folk tradition provides us with patterns for just about any performance style we would wish to adopt. Just as one tradition calls for a restrained telling style and a passive audience, in

---

1. Roger Abrahams, *A Singer and Her Songs: Alameda Riddle's Book of Ballads* (Baton Rouge: Louisiana State University Press, 1970), p. 153.
2. MacEdward Leach, "The Singer or the Song" in *Singers and Storytellers*, ed. Mody C. Boatright (Dallas, Texas: Southern Methodist University Press, 1961), p. 37.

many cultures, certain genres of storytelling involve the audience directly in the telling. The audience may chant refrains, sing, even dance as the story flows along.

Diane Wolkstein's *Magic Orange Tree* offers several examples of a responsive audience in action. Of a telling of "Horse and Toad" she says: "Elmir Innocent, a young woman of twenty, told the story of Horse and Toad's race in a clear, engaging, dramatic manner at Masson. When she sang Toad's song, she provocatively moved her hips from side to side. When she sang Horse's song, she hardly moved, holding her head in the air. The audience joined her full-heartedly. I, too, was singing Toad's song along with everyone."[3] The Haitian teller involves his audience from the onset by calling "Cric?" If the audience wants to hear the tale they respond with a resounding "CRACK!" The heartiness of the audience's "Crack" is an indicator of their eagerness to hear this teller. It is an excellent technique for sounding out audience response before one launches into a telling.

Several genres of African oral performance incorporate audience response. Daniel Biebuyck says of African epic performances that "The audience responds with dialogue and praises, refrain singing and dances, handclapping and percussion. The epic performance is an outstanding example of collective rejoicing..."[4]

In a culture in which storytelling is a recurring event, the audience will have its own repertoire of chants and songs which form a part of the stories. The audience has likely heard these same stories many times. They know where to come in with a chant, where to break into song. They come to enjoy repeated performance under the leadership of a skillful teller. Knowing the traditional patterning and form of a tale, the audience can easily assume its participatory role, even with a tale heard for the first time.

---

3. Diane Wolkstein, *The Magic Orange Tree and Other Haitian Folktales* (New York: Alfred A. Knopf, 1978), p. 30-31.
4. Daniel Biebuyck, "The African Heroic Epic" in *The Heroic Epic*, ed. Felix J. Oinas (Bloomington: Indiana University Press, 1978). p. 352.

You will find that your audiences respond similarly. If you have opportunity to tell repeatedly to the same group, they will soon follow your participation cues easily as you share new tales. And they will love to take part again in the performance of favorites from your repertoire.

Though many storytelling events include audience participation, few tale texts include clues which will enable the library storyteller to reproduce such audience-involved tellings. Collections such as Moses Serwadda's *Songs and Stories from Uganda* and Adjai Robinson's *Singing Tales from Africa* do provide music and some clues for audience involvement. Films such as *Mapagandere, the Great Baboon* let us see an audience in active participation. With a little help, we can recreate the delight of an audience-involved telling.

To learn more about storytelling in folk settings, read Anne Pellowski's *The World of Storytelling* (Bowker, 1977) and consult its excellent bibliography.

PART III: SOURCES

RESEARCHING TALE VARIANTS

You may find it useful in your tale preparation to research other variants of the tale. Folklorists classify tales by type and motif, and once you have learned the type and motif numbers assigned to your tale, you can readily locate other variants by searching through folktale indexes.

The Types of the Folktale, prepared by Antti Aarne and Stith Thompson, assigns one type number to each tale. Stith Thompson complements this type system with his *Motif-Index*, assigning a motif number to each part of a tale. Cinderella, for example, is Type 510, but includes many motifs such as R221 *Heroine's three-fold flight from ball*; H36.1 *Slipper test*; F823.2 *Glass shoes*; and F861.3.2 *Carriage from pumpkin*.

Many folktale collections include type and motif numbers in their tale notes. If your collection does not provide type and motif numbers, you may be able to discover the tale's motif number by searching in MacDonald's *Storyteller's Sourcebook* or Stith Thompson's *Motif-Index of Folk-Literature*. Both have extensive subject indexes, and MacDonald includes a tale title index. These motif-indexes often include a tale type number in their tale descriptions as well.

Once you have discovered your tale's motif and type numbers, it is possible to trace the tale in any of the several regional indexes. Most of these specialized indexes are available only at large university libraries or in the main libraries of large metropolitan areas. You may have to spend some time ferreting them out and learning how to use them. Another pitfall of folktale research is the fact the many of the collections to which these indexes refer us are not available locally. Keep in mind, however, that many of these sources are available through your local library via inter-library loan.

Once you have located your motif or type number in an index, take time to browse a bit in the index. Note that these indexes are set up in such a way that related tale material is displayed together. Scanning the motif or type numbers located near your given number may turn up several related tales.

Begin your tale research with MacDonald's *Storyteller's Sourcebook*. This indexes 556 children's folktale collections and 389 picture books. Many of these sources will be available locally in your school or public libraries. Once you have whetted your appetite for folktale study with these accessible materials, you may want to tackle some of the more formidable tools listed in the bibliography below.

TYPE AND MOTIF INDEXES FOR FOLKTALE RESEARCH

Aarne, Antti, and Stith Thompson. *The Types of the Folktale.* Folklore Fellows Communications, no. 184. Helsinki: Suomalainen Tiedeakatemia, 1973.

Standard index used by folklorists throughout the world to classify folktales. Each tale is assigned one type number.

Baughman, Ernest W. *Type and Motif-Index of the Folktales of England and North America.* Indiana University Folklore Series, no. 20. The Hague: Mouton & Co., 1966.

Contains type and motif indexes for folktales "in the English language tradition" from England and North America. No American Indian materials are included. A few Spanish American tales are included. Tale annotations make this a useful browsing tool for anyone studying the folktale traditions of the United States.

Clarke, Kenneth Wendell. "A Motif-Index of the Folktales of Culture—Area V, West Africa." (Ph.D. dissertation. Indiana University, 1958.) Ann Arbor, Michigan: University Micro films International, 590 pages.

Not available in most libraries, but can be ordered from University Microfilms.

Hansen, Terence L. *The Types of the Folktale in Cuba, Puerto Rico, the Dominican Republic, and Spanish South America.* University of California Publications, Folklore Studies, no. 8. Berkeley: University of California Press, 1957.

Ikeda, Hiroko. *A Type and Motif Index of Japanese Folk-Literature*. Folklore Fellows Communications, no. 209. Helsinki: Suomalainen Tiedeakatemia, 1971.

Most of the primary sources to which reference is made are in Japanese.

Kirtley, Bacil Fleming. *A Motif-Index of Traditional Polynesian Narratives*. Honolulu: University of Hawaii, 1971.

MacDonald, Margaret Read. *The Storyteller's Sourcebook: A Subject, Title, and Motif Index to Folklore Collections for Children*. Detroit: Neal-Schuman/Gale Research, 1982.

Indexes 556 folktale collections and 389 picture books. Tales are listed by subject, title, and motif number. Brief annotations and cross references to related motifs are included.

O'Suilleabhain, Sean, and Reider Th. Christiansen. *The Types of the Irish Folktale*. Folklore Fellows Communications, no. 188. Helsinki: Suomalainen Tiedeakatemia, 1963.

Thompson, Stith. *Motif-Index of Folk-Literature*. 6 vols. rev. ed. Bloomington: Indiana University Press, 1955-1958.

This six-volume set is found in most large public libraries and college libraries. Thompson may be approached through its excellent subject index. All motif-indexes listed here are patterned after Stith Thompson. Since none of the other indexes include subject access, you will have to use Thompson or MacDonald to locate motif numbers before carrying your research into other indexes.

BUILDING BACKGROUND IN THE FOLKTALE

Briggs, Katharine M. *A Dictionary of British Folk-Tales in the English Language*. 4 vols. Bloomington: Indiana University Press, 1970.

Sample texts from a wide range of British folktales. Type and motif numbers and one-line tale notes are given for each tale. A type index is included.

Clarkson, Atelia and Gilbert B. Cross. *World Folktales: A Scribner Resource Collection.* New York: Scribner's, 1980.

Sixty-six tales with excellent comparative notes. Motif and type indexes included.

Dorson, Richard M., general editor. Folktales of the World series. Chicago: University of Chicago Press.

Each title in this series is devoted to the folktales of a particular country and compiled by a noted scholar. In a forward to each volume, Dorson discusses the history of folktale research in that country. An introduction by the collection's author discusses the tale material in the collection and the folktale tradition of the country. Notes are provided for each tale, and motif and type indexes are included. Most of the volumes are available in paperback. Listed below are some of the titles in the series:

> Briggs, Katharine M. and Ruth L. Tongue, editors. *Folktales of England* (1965).
>
> Christiansen, Reidar Th., editor. *Folktales of Norway* (1964).
>
> Dégh, Linda, editor. *Folktales of Hungary* (1965).
>
> Eberhard, Wolfram, editor. *Folktales of China* (1965).
>
> Massignon, Geneviève, editor. *Folktales of France* (1968).
>
> Megas, Georgios A., editor. *Folktales of Greece* (1970).
>
> Noy, Dov, editor. *Folktales of Israel* (1963).
>
> O'Sullivan, Sean, editor. *Folktales of Ireland* (1966).
>
> Paredes, Americo, editor. *Folktales of Mexico* (1970).
>
> Pino-Saavedra, Yolando, editor. *Folktales of Chile* (1968).
>
> Ranke, Kurt, editor. *Folktales of Germany* (1966).
>
> Seki, Keigo, editor. *Folktales of Japan* (1963).
>
> Shamy, Hasan M., editor. *Folktales of Egypt* (1979).

Pellowski, Anne. *The World of Storytelling.* New York: R. R. Bowker, 1977.

Discussion of storytelling traditions around the world, including a section on public library storytellers.

Thompson, Stith. *The Folktale*. New York: Holt, Rinehart and Winston, 1946.

Comparative discussion of folktales. Includes motif and type indexes. Extensive bibliography of folktale studies arranged by country.

COLLECTIONS WITH TEXTS CLOSE TO THEIR ORAL ORIGINS

I include here only collections whose texts are not far removed from their original oral tellings. These are texts that will flow back into an oral style with relative ease.

Chase, Richard, *Grandfather Tales*. American-English folktales selected and edited by Richard Chase. Illustrated by Berkeley Williams, Jr. Boston: Houghton Mifflin, 1948.

Tales collected in North Carolina, Virginia, and Kentucky. Chase gives the names of his informants and includes brief tale notes. Chase is a storyteller himself and keeps his tales close to an oral style.

———. *The Jack Tales*. Appendix compiled by Herbert Halpert. Illustrated by Berkeley Williams, Jr. Boston: Houghton Mifflin, 1943.

Similar to *Grandfather Tales*. All tales are about Jack and his adventures with giants, beanstalks, the king's daughter, etc. European tale material retold in an Appalachian idiom.

Jacobs, Joseph. *English Folk and Fairy Tales*. Illustrated by John D. Batten. New York: Putnam, n.d.

Tales collected by late nineteenth century folklore collectors in the English countryside. Jacobs includes information about the tellers and tale notes. These tales are set down much as they were originally spoken. They retell with ease and have been favorites of storytellers for years.

———. *More English Folk and Fairy Tales*. Illustrated by John D. Batten. New York: Putnam, n.d.

202

Robinson, Adjai. *Singing Tales of Africa*. Illustrated by Christine Price. New York: Scribner's, 1974.

Singing tales from Sierra Leone, Nigeria, and Ghana retold by a native of Sierra Leone who is himself a storyteller. Musical notation and words for songs included.

Scofield, Elizabeth. *Hold Tight, Stick Tight: A Collection of Japanese Folk Tales*. Illustrated by K. Wakana. Tokyo: Kodansha, 1966.

Six short Japanese mukashi-banashi tales. Author was a school teacher storyteller in Japan for three years, and she retains the onomatopoetic phrases of the Japanese originals.

———. *A Fox in One Bite and Other Tasty Tales form Japan*. Illustrated by K. Wakana. Tokyo: Kodansha, 1965.

Six tales of magic badgers and foxes.

Serwadda, W. Moses. *Songs and Stories from Uganda*. Transcribed and edited by Hewitt Pantaleoni. Illustrated by Leo and Diane Dillon. New York: Crowell, 1974.

Songs, which are an integral part of these stories, are included with musical notation and words in both Luganda and English.

Tashjian, Virginia A. *Juba This and Juba That: Story Hour Stretches for Large or Small Groups*. Illustrated by Victoria de Larrea. Boston: Little, Brown, 1969.

Storytime stretches and short stories with audience participation.

———. *With a Deep Sea Smile: Story Hour Stretches for Large or Small Groups*. Illustrated by Rosemary Wells. Boston: Little, Brown, 1974.

More of the above.

Tedlock, Dennis. *Finding the Center: Narrative Poetry of the Zuni Indians*. Translated by Dennis Tedlock. From performances in the Zuni by Andrew Peynetsa and Walter Sanchez. New York: Dial, 1972.

Tales transcribed in an ethnopoetic format that will help the reader reproduce to some extent the oral style of the teller. Includes notes about the tellers. Phrases and ideas unique to the

Zuni context are explained. Though this collection is not prepared with children in mind, several of the tales could be used with children.

Tracey, Hugh. *The Lion on the Path and Other African Stories.* Illustrated by Eric Byrd. Music transcribed by Andrew Tracey. New York: Praeger, c. 1967, 1968.

Collected by a British anthropologist working in Rhodesia. Musical notation included. For filmed tellings of two of these tales see *Mapagandere: The Great Baboon* and *The Dancing Lion* in the bibliography under Films/Videotapes.

Wolkstein, Diane. *The Magic Orange Tree and other Haitian Folktales.* Illustrated by Elsa Henriquez. New York: Knopf, 1978.

Storyteller Diane Wolkstein traveled to Haiti to record these tellings which retell with ease. She includes musical notation and words in Haitian Creole and English. She speaks of her tale-collecting experiences and tells something about the setting and the teller for most tales. This collection is not to be missed.

THE PICTURE BOOK AS A STORY SOURCE

The pictures will help you remember the story. First, tell the tale without the pictures. Then, show the illustrations or display the book where the children can pore over the pictures on their own. Most of these titles also work well read aloud as picture books. Some are so stunningly illustrated that one can hardly bear not to show the illustrations as one tells.

Aardema, Verna. *Who's in Rabbit's House?* A Masai Tale. Illustrated by Leo and Diane Dillon. New York: Dial, 1977.

_____. *Why Mosquitoes Buzz in People's Ears.* A West African Tale. Illustrated by Leo and Diane Dillon. New York: Dial, 1975.

_____. *Half-a-Ball-of-Kenki.* An Ashanti Tale. Illustrated by Diane Stanley Zuromskis. New York: Frederick Warne, 1979.

Bang, Betsy. *The Old Woman and the Red Pumpkin.* A Bengali Folktale. Illustrated by Molly Garrett Bang. New York: Macmillan, 1975.

_____. *Wiley and the Hairy Man.* Adapted from an American Folktale. Illustrated by Molly Garrett Bang. New York: Macmillan, 1976. An I CAN READ book.

Brown, Marcia. *The Three Billy Goats Gruff.* Illustrated by author. New York: Harcourt, Brace & World, 1957.

Buffet, Guy and Pam. *Pua Pua Lena Lena and the Magic Kiha-Pu.* Edited by Ruth Tabrah. Illustrated by Guy Buffet. New York: Weatherhill (Island Heritage), 1972.

_____. *The Adventures of Kama Pua'a.* Edited by Ruth Tabrah. Illustrated by Guy Buffet. Island Heritage, 1972.

Dayrell, Elphinstone. *Why the Sun and the Moon Live in the Sky.* An African Folktale. Illustrated by Blair Lent. Boston: Houghton Mifflin, 1968.

De Paola, Tomie. *The Cat on the Dovrefell: A Christmas Tale.* Translated from the Norse by Sir George Webbe Dasent. Illustrated by Tomie de Paola. New York: G. P. Putnam's, 1979.

Duff, Maggie. *Rum Pum Pum.* A folktale from India. Illustrated by Jose Aruego and Ariane Dewey. New York: Macmillan, 1978.

Galdone, Joanna. *The Little Girl and the Big Bear.* Illustrated by Paul Galdone. New York: Houghton Mifflin/Clarion Books, 1980.

_____. *The Tailypo: A Ghost Story.* Illustrated by Paul Galdone. New York: Seabury, 1977.

_____. *The Gingerbread Boy.* Illustrated by author. New York: Houghton Mifflin/Clarion Books, 1975.

_____. *Henny Penny.* Illustrated by author. New York: Seabury, 1968.

_____. *King of the Cats.* A Ghost Story by Joseph Jacobs. Retold and illustrated by Paul Galdone. New York: Houghton Mifflin/Clarion Books, 1980.

———. *The Three Wishes*. Illustrated by author. New York: McGraw-Hill, 1961.

———. *What's in Fox's Sack?* An Old English Tale. Illustrated by author. New York: Houghton Mifflin/Clarion Books, 1982.

Ginsburg, Mirra. *The Strongest One of All*. Based on a Caucasian folktale. Illustrated by Jose Aruego and Ariane Dewey. New York: Greenwillow, 1977.

———. *Two Greedy Bears*. Adapted from a Hungarian folktale. Illustrated by Jose Aruego and Ariane Dewey. New York: Macmillan, 1976.

Haley, Gail E. *A Story, A Story*. An African Tale. Illustrated by author. New York: Atheneum, 1970.

Hardendorff, Jeanne B. *Slip! Slop! Gobble!* Illustrated by Emily McCully. Philadelphia: J. B. Lippincott, 1970.

———. *The Bed Just So*. Illustrated by Lisl Weil. New York: Four Winds, 1975.

Harper, Wilhelmina. *The Gunniwolf*. Illustrated by William Wiesner. New York: E.P. Dutton, 1967.

Hirsh, Marilyn. *Could Anything Be Worse? A Yiddish Tale*. Illustrated by author. New York: Holiday House, 1974.

Jacobs, Joseph. *Johnny-Cake*. Illustrated by Emma Brock. New York: Putnam, 1933.

———. *King of the Cats*. Illustrated by Paul Galdone. Boston: Houghton Mifflin, 1980.

Jameson, Cynthia. *Catofy the Clever*. Adapted from a Russian Folktale. Illustrated by Wallace Tripp. New York: Coward-McCann, and Geoghegan, 1972.

Kent, Jack. *The Fat Cat*. A Danish Folktale. Translated and illustrated by author. New York: Parents' Magazine Press, 1971.

Leodhas, Sorce Nic. *Always Room for One More*. Illustrated by Nonny Hogrogian. New York: Holt, Rinehart & Winston, 1965.

Lefévre, Felicite. *The Cock, the Mouse and the Little Red Hen*. Illustrated by Tony Sarg. Philadelphia: Macrae-Smith, n.d.

McDermott, Gerald. *The Voyage of Osiris: A Myth of Ancient Egypt.* Illustrated by author. New York: Windmill Books and E. P. Dutton, 1977.

_____. *Arrow to the Sun. A Pueblo Indian Tale.* Illustrated by author. New York: Viking, 1974.

McGovern, Ann. *Too Much Noise.* Illustrated by Simms Taback. Boston: Houghton Mifflin, 1967.

Mohan, Beverly. *Punia and the King of the Sharks.* Illustrated by Don Bolognese. Chicago: Follett, 1964.

Mosel, Arlene. *The Funny Little Woman.* Illustrated by Blair Lent. New York: E. P. Dutton, 1972.

Ness, Evaline. *Tom Tit Tot: An English Folk Tale.* New York: Scribner's, 1965.

Sawyer, Ruth. *Journey Cake Ho!* Illustrated by Robert McCloskey. New York: Viking, 1956.

Schneider, Rex. *The Wide-Mouthed Frog.* Illustrated by author. Owings Mills, Maryland: Stemmer House, 1980.

Seuling, Barbara. *The Teeny-Tiny Woman: An Old English Ghost Tale.* New York: Viking, 1976.

Shannon, George. *Dance Away.* Illustrated by Jose Aruego and Ariane Dewey. New York: Greenwillow Books, 1982.

_____. *Lizard's Song.* Illustrated by Jose Aruego and Ariane Dewey. New York: Greenwillow, 1981.

_____. *The Piney Woods Peddler.* Illustrated by Nancy Tafuri. New York: Greenwillow, 1981.

Skurzynski, Gloria. *The Magic Pumpkin.* Illustrated by Rocco Negri. New York: Four Winds, 1971.

Stobbs, William. *Henny Penny.* Illustrated by author. Chicago: Follett, 1970.

Toye, William. *How Summer Came to Canada.* Illustrated by Elizabeth Cleaver. New York: Henry Z. Walck, 1969.

_____. *The Mountain Goats of Temlaham.* Illustrated by Elizabeth Cleaver. New York: Henry Z. Walck, 1969.

Tresselt, Alvin. *The Mitten!* An Old Ukrainian Folktale.

Adapted from the version by E. Rachev. Illustrated by Yaroslava. New York: Lothrop, Lee & Shephard, 1964.

Wahl, Jan. *Drakestail.* Illustrated by Byron Barton. New York: Greenwillow, 1978.

Withers, Carl. *The Tale of a Black Cat.* Illustrated by Alan Cober. New York: Holt, Rinehart & Winston, 1966.

————. *The Wild Ducks and the Goose.* Illustrated by Alan Cober. New York: Holt, Rinehart & Winston, 1968.

Yoda, Junichi. *The Rolling Rice Ball.* Translated by Alvin Tresselt. Illustrated by Saburo Watanabe. New York: Parents' Magazine Press, 1968.

Young, Ed. *The Terrible Nung Gwama.* A Chinese Folktale. Adapted from the retelling by Leslie Bonnet. Illustrated by author. Collins & World in cooperation with the U.S. Committee for UNICEF, 1978.

Young, Ed with Hilary Beckett. *The Rooster's Horns.* Illustrated by Ed Young. New York: Collins & World, 1978.

Zemach, Margo. *It Could Always Be Worse.* New York: Farrar, Straus, and Giroux, 1976.

MEDIA FOLKTELLINGS

One of the best ways to acquire new tales is to listen to other tellers. This enables you to avoid a stifling printed text and keep the living oral-aural-oral tradition flowing. Possibly only a few of these tales will suit your own style, but all are worth hearing for the delightful variety of folk telling they present.

RECORDINGS:

African Story-Songs. Told and sung by Abraham Dumisani Maraire. Seattle: University of Washington Press, 1969.

Eight Shona story-songs, recorded by Rhodesian Abraham Dumisani Maraire, backed by a group of instrumentalists and singers trained by him. Song texts are provided on the record jacket. Useful both for classroom listening and as a storytelling source.

Alaskan Eskimo Songs and Stories. Compiled and recorded by Lorraine Donoghue Koranda. Illustrated by Robert Mayokok. Published for the Alaska Festival of Music in Cooperation with BP Alaska Inc. by the University of Washington Press, Seattle and London, 1966, 1972.

Contains several stories that include songs and several story-songs. Notations for the songs and transliterations of the song texts are included. Several of these tales could be adapted for storytime use, though it would be very difficult to reproduce the songs. This is an excellent record for building background in Eskimo folklore. The charming tellings of Maggie Lind would make especially good classroom listening.

Richard Chase tells three "Jack Tales" from the Southern Appalachians. Folk-Legacy FTA-6. Sharon, Connecticut: Folk-Legacy.

Folktale collector Richard Chase has honed his own storytelling skills through years of performances. His tellings of three Jack tales here have a relaxed folk quality.

The Folktellers: Tales to Grow On. Told by The Folktellers featuring Barbara Freeman and Connie Regan. Weston Woods, WW711, 1981.

This is one of several albums produced by the The Folktellers. It includes examples of audience participation tales and tandem telling.

Ray Hicks of Beech Mountain, North Carolina, Telling Four Traditional "Jack Tales." Folk-Legacy FTA-14. Sharon, Connecticut: Folk-Legacy, 1963.

Four Jack tales told by North Carolina mountain farmer, Ray Hicks. Booklet accompanying record describes the home setting in which the tales were recorded and gives some background information about the teller and his dialect. Transcribed tale texts are included.

A Storytelling Sampler. Featuring storytellers from the National Storytelling Festival in historic Jonesborough, Tennessee. Produced by the National Association for the Preservation and Perpetuation of Storytelling, 1978.

Eleven storytellers with a variety of telling styles, most of them highly individual and not easily imitable. This is particularly interesting as a sampler of folktelling styles. Includes David Holt, Doc McConnell, Ed Bell, Henry Hatch, Barbara Freeman, Connie Regan, Kathryn Windham, Jackie Torrence, Harriette Allen, Marshall Dodge, and Diane Wolkstein. This is only one of several storytelling samplers produced by NAPPS at its annual storytelling festivals.

I have listed here only recordings which give examples of traditional tellers in action, or recordings which for the most part contain tales easily imitable by beginning storytellers. Other storytelling artists who may be heard on record/tape include Anne Pellowski, Nancy Schimmel, Heather Forest, David Holt, Laura Sims, Jackie Torrence, and Jay O'Callahan. Caedmon, Spoken Arts, and other recording labels feature artists reading from folktale collections, which may be helpful as well.

FILMS AND VIDEOTAPES:

The Dancing Lion. FilmFair, 1978. 10½ min.

Ethnomusicologist Andrew Tracey tells this Rhodesian tale to children in an African setting. In a prologue he discusses the use of musical instruments within the tale. The tale is told using mime, chant, music, and in both English and native language.

Mapandangare — the Great Baboon. FilmFair, 1978. 9 min.

See Review for *The Dancing Lion* above. The text for Mapandangare appears in Hugh Tracey's *The Lion on the Path* (Praeger, 1967).

Jay O'Callahan: A Master Class in Storytelling. Vineyard Video Productions, 1983. 33 min. color. Film or video.

Excellent advice from a master storyteller.

Stories Everywhere. National Association for the Preservation and Perpetuation of Storytelling and Adair Films, 1982. 26 min. Film or video.

Includes four storytelling settings: the informal anecdote told in conversation (Barbara Hughes); traditional storytelling (Ray Hicks); classroom storytelling (Jackie Torrence); the story concert for all ages (Jackie Torrence and Doc McConnell).

There's Something about a Story. 27 min. color. Distributor: Wm. D. Stoneback, 6 Cobble Hill Rd., Westport, CT 06880, 1966.

Ten library storytellers with varied styles are filmed telling to children in libraries and parks. Produced by the Dayton, Ohio, and Montgomery County Public Libraries.

For more information on storytelling recordings and videos consult the review section of *The National Storytelling Journal.* (National Association for the Preservation and Perpetuation of Storytelling, P.O. Box 112, Jonesborough, Tennessee, 37659.)

BASIC BOOKS FOR THE BEGINNING STORYTELLER

Baker, Augusta and Ellin Greene. *Storytelling: Art and Technique.* New York: R. R. Bowker, 1977.

Useful advice on selecting, preparing, and presenting the story. Includes notes on program planning, publicity, inservice workshops, and serving children with special needs.

Bauer, Caroline Feller. *Handbook for Storytellers.* Chicago: American Library Association, 1977. Storytelling advice, and suggestions for program building through use of media, magic, puppetry, music, etc. A great idea sourcebook.

_____. *This Way to Books.* New York: H. W. Wilson Company, 1983.

More storytelling suggestions and tons of ideas for introducing literature to children. Elementary teachers and librarians should not fail to examine this remarkable sourcebook.

_____. *Celebrations.* New York: H. W. Wilson Company, 1985.

Read-aloud holiday and theme book programs.

Pellowski, Anne. *The Story Vine: A Source Book of Unusual and Easy-to-Tell Stories from Around the World*. New York: Macmillan, 1984.

A collection of string stories, drawing stories, doll stories, fingerplay stories, riddles, and musical stories with notes on their use. Included here because these short tales are easy for the beginning teller.

Sawyer, Ruth. *The Way of the Storyteller*. New York: Viking, c. 1942, 1962.

This classic volume offers inspiration and advice, and should be read by every storyteller-in-training.

Schimmel, Nancy. *Just Enough to Make a Story: A Sourcebook for Storytelling*. Berkeley: Sisters' Choice Press, 2nd ed., 1982.

Brief advice and some favorite stories.

Shedlock, Marie. *The Art of the Storyteller*. New York: Dover, 1951.

A classic source first published in 1915.

For a more extensive bibliography of materials about storytelling see:

Storytelling: Readings/Bibliographies/Resources. Prepared by an ad hoc committee of the Association for Library Service to Children, American Library Association. Chicago: American Library Association, 1978.

BIBLIOGRAPHY OF WORKS CONSULTED

Aarne, Antti. *Die Tiere auf der Wanderschaft*. Folklore Fellows Communications, no. 11. Helsinki: Suomalainen Tiedeakatemia, 1913.

Aarne, Antti and Stith Thompson. *The Types of the Folktale: A Classification and Bibliography*. Folklore Fellows Communications, no. 184. Helsinki: Suomalainen Tiedeakatemia, 1973.

Alaskan Eskimo Songs and Stories. Compiled and recorded by Lorraine Donaghue Koranda. University of Washington Press, 1972. (UWP 902)

Alcheringa. Boston University, 1970-1980.

Ambrus, Victor G. *The Little Cockerel*. New York: Harcourt, Brace & World, 1968.

Anderson, Paul. *The Boy and the Blind Storyteller*. New York: W. R. Scott, 1964.

Baker, Augusta and Ellin Greene. *Storytelling: Art & Technique*. New York: R. R. Bowker, 1977.

Bang, Garrett. *Men from the Village Deep in the Mountains*. New York: Macmillan, 1973.

Bang, Molly. *The Goblin's Giggle and Other Stories*. New York: Scribner's, 1973.

Barnes, Walter A. *West Virginia Folklore*. V.3, 1952.

Bebel, Heinrich. *Schwänke*. Edited by A. Wesselski. Munich: G. Müller, 1907.

Beckwith, Martha. *Hawaiian Mythology*. Honolulu: University of Hawaii Press, 1970.

Bell, Corydon. *John Rattling Gourd of Big Cove: A Collection of Cherokee Indian Legends*. New York: Macmillan, 1955.

Belting, Natalia. *The Long-Tailed Bear and Other Indian Legends*. Indianapolis: Bobbs-Merrill, 1961.

_____. *Our Fathers Had Powerful Songs*. New York: E. P. Dutton, 1974.

Ben-Amos, Dan, editor. *Folklore Genres.* Austin: University of Texas Press, 1976.

Biebuyck, Daniel. "The African Heroic Epic." *See* Oinas, Felix J.

Boas, Franz. *See* Parsons, Elsie Clews.

Bolte, J. and G. Polivka. Anmerkungen zu den Kinder- und Hausmärchen, II. Leipzig: Theodor Weicher, 1915.

Briggs, Katharine. *A Dictionary of British Folk-tales.* Bloomington: Indiana University Press, 1970.

Bro, Margueritte. *How the Mouse Deer Became King.* Garden City, New York: Doubleday, 1966.

Brocket, Eleanor. *Burmese and Thai Fairy Tales.* Chicago: Follet, c. 1965.

Brown, Dee. *Tepee Tales of the American Indian.* New York: Holt, Rinehart & Winston, 1979.

Carpenter, Frances. *African Wonder Tales.* Garden City, New York: Doubleday, 1963.

―――. *Tales of a Korean Grandmother.* Garden City, New York: Doubleday, 1947.

Carrick, Valery. *Picture Folk-Tales.* New York: Dover, 1967.

Chase, Richard. *Grandfather Tales: American-English Folk Tales.* Boston: Houghton Mifflin, 1948.

―――. *The Jack Tales.* Boston: Houghton Mifflin, 1943.

―――. *See* "Jack and the Robbers."

Clarke, Kenneth Wendell. "A Motif-Index for the Folktales of Culture―Area V, West Africa." (Ph.D. dissertation. Indiana University, 1958.)

Clarkson, Atelia and Gilbert B. Cross. *World Folktales: A Scribner Resource Collection.* New York: Scribner's, 1980.

Colum, Padraic. *Legends of Hawaii.* New Haven: Yale U. Press, 1937.

―――. *Stone of Victory and Other Tales.* New York: McGraw-Hill, 1966.

Colwell, Eileen. *The Magic Umbrella and Other Stories for Telling*. New York: McKay, 1976.

Cothran, Jean. *The Magic Calabash: Folk Tales from America's Islands and Alaska*. New York: McKay, 1956.

Courlander, Harold. *People of the Short Blue Corn: Tales and Legends of the Hopi Indians*. New York: Harcourt Brace Jovanovich, 1970.

_____. *Ride with the Sun: An Anthology of Folk Tales and Stories from the United Nations*. New York: Whittlesey House, 1955.

Cox, John Harrington. "Negro Tales from West Virginia," *Journal of American Folk-Lore*, LVII, No. 186, 1934.

Curry, Jane Louise. *Down from the Lonely Mountain: California Indian Tales*. New York: Harcourt, Brace & World, 1965.

DeVissen, M. W. "The Fox and Badger in Japanese Folklore" in *Transactions of the Asiatic Society of Japan*, XXXVI, Part 3, 1908.

Dobbs, Rose. *Once Upon a Time: Twenty Cheerful Tales to Read and Tell*. New York: Random House, 1950.

Dolch, Edward W. and Marguerite P. *Pueblo Stories*. Champaign, Illinois: Garrard, 1956.

Dorson, Richard. *Folk Legends of Japan*. Rutledge, Vermont: Tuttle, 1962.

Duff, Maggie. *Rum Pum Pum: A Folktale from India*. New York: Macmillan, 1978.

The Eskimo of Siberia. Publication of the Jessup North Pacific Expedition. Vol. 8, Part 3. Leiden and New York, 1913.

Fitzgerald, Burdette S. *World Tales for Creative Dramatics and Storytelling*. Englewood Cliffs, New Jersey: Prentice-Hall, 1962.

Floating Eagle Feather, ed. *As One Is So One Sees: Stories, Poems and Epigrams*. Denver, Colorado: Renaissance Artists and Writers Association, 1983.

Folktellers. *Tales to Grow on*. Told by The Folktellers (featuring Barbara Freeman and Connie Regan). Weston Woods WW 711, 1981.

Gilham, Charles. *Beyond the Clapping Mountains: Eskimo Stories from Alaska*. New York: Macmillan, 1943.

Ginsburg, Mirra. *The Lazies: Tales of the People of Russia*. New York: Macmillan, 1973.

———. *The Magic Stove*. New York: Coward-McCann, 1983.

Gittins, Anne. *Tales from the South Pacific Islands*. Owings Mills, Maryland: Stemmer House, 1977.

Halliwell-Phillipps, James Orchard. *Popular Rhymes and Nursery Tales*. London: John Russell Smith, 1849. Reissued by Singing Tree Press, 1968.

Hardendorff, Jeanne. *The Little Cock*. Philadelphia: Lippincott, 1969.

Harper, Wilhelmina. *The Gunniwolf*. New York: Dutton, 1967.

Harris, Christie. *Once Upon a Totem*. New York: Atheneum, 1963.

Harris, Joel Chandler. *Nights with Uncle Remus*. Boston and New York: Houghton Mifflin, 1883.

Haviland, Virginia. *North American Legends*. New York and Cleveland: Collins, 1979.

Heady, Eleanor B. *Sage Smoke: Tales of the Shoshoni-Bannock Indians*. Chicago: Follett, 1973.

Hearn, Lafcadio. *The Boy Who Drew Cats*. New York: Macmillan, 1963.

Holding, James. *The Sky-Eater and Other South Sea Tales*. New York: Abelard-Schuman, 1956.

Hutchinson, Veronica S. *Candle-Light Stories*. New York: Minton, Balch, 1927.

"Jack and the Robbers" (told by Richard Chase). Pied Piper Productions, 1975. Color film. 15 min.

Jacobs, Joseph. *English Folk and Fairy Tales*. New York: G. P. Putnam's, n.d.

———. *Indian Fairy Tales*. New York: G. P. Putnam's, n.d.

_____. *More English Fairy Tales*. New York: G. P. Putnam's, 1894.

Jagendorf, Moritz A. *Noodlehead Stories from around the World*. New York: Vanguard, 1957.

Johnston, Clifton. *The Birch-Tree Fairy Book*. Boston: Little, Brown, 1906.

Judson, Katharine B. *Myths and Legends of the Mississippi Valley and the Great Lakes*. Chicago: A. B. McClurg, 1914.

Keithahn, Edward L. *Igloo Tales*. United States Indian Service, 1950.

Kirtley, Bacil F. *A Motif-Index of Traditional Polynesian Narratives*. Honolulu: University of Hawaii Press, 1971.

Koch-Grünberg, Theodor. *Indianermärchen aus Südamerica*. Jena: Eugen Diederichs, 1927.

Leach, Maria. *Noodles, Nitwits, and Numskulls*. Cleveland: World, 1961.

Leekley, Thomas B. *The World of Manabozho: Tales of the Chippewa Indians*. New York: Vanguard, 1965.

Lowe, Patricia Tracy. *The Little Horse of Seven Colors and Other Portuguese Folk Tales*. New York: World, 1970.

Lowrimore, Burton. "Six California Tales," *California Folklore Quarterly*. V.4, 1945.

MacDonald, Margaret Read. *The Storyteller's Sourcebook: A Subject, Title, and Motif Index to Children's Folklore Collections*. Detroit: Neal-Schuman/Gale Research, 1982.

Manning-Sanders, Ruth. *Tortoise Tales*. Nashville, Tennessee: Nelson, 1972.

Masey, Mary Lou. *Stories of the Steppes: Kazakh Folktales*. New York: McKay, 1968.

Matson, Emerson N. *Legends of the Great Chiefs*. Nashville, Tennessee: Nelson, 1972.

Melzack, Ronald. *The Day Tuk Became a Hunter and Other Eskimo Stories*. New York: Dodd, Mead, 1967.

Mohan, Beverly. *Punia and the King of the Sharks*. Chicago: Follett, 1964.

Mooney, James. "Myths of the Cherokee" in *Nineteenth Annual Report of the Bureau of American Ethnology...1897-98*. Washington: Government Printing Office, 1900.

Mosel, Arlene. *The Funny Little Woman*. New York: E. P. Dutton, 1972.

Nahmad, H. M. *The Peasant and the Donkey: Tales of the Near and Middle East*. New York: Walck, 1968.

Oinas, Felix J., editor. *Heroic Epic and Saga: An Introduction to the World's Great Folk Epics*. Bloomington: Indiana University Press, 1978.

Okeke, Uche. *Tales of Land of Death: Igbo Folk Tales*. New York: Doubleday, 1971.

Opie, Iona and Peter. *The Classic Fairy Tales*. London: Oxford University Press, 1974.

Parsons, Elsie Clews. "Navaho Folk Tales" in *Journal of American Folk-Lore*, Vol. XXXVI, No. 142, 1923.

———. "Pueblo-Indian Folk-Tales, Probably of Spanish Provenience" in *Journal of American Folklore*, Vol. XXXI, No. 70, 1918.

Parsons, Elsie Clews and Franz Boas. "Spanish Tales from Laguna and Zuñi, New Mexico" in *Journal of American Folklore*, Vol. XXXIII, No. 127, 1920.

Pellowski, Anne. *The Story Vine: A Source Book of Unusual and Easy-to-Tell Stories from Around the World*. New York: Macmillan, 1984.

Robinson, Adjai. *Singing Tales of Africa*. New York: Scribner's 1974.

Robinson, Gail and Douglas Hill. *Coyote the Trickster. Legends of the North American Indians*. New York: Crane Russack, 1975.

Roessel, Robert A., Jr. and Dillon Platero. *Coyote Stories of the Navajo People*. Rough Rock, Arkansas: Navajo Curriculum Center Press, 1974.

Running, Corinne. *When Coyote Walked the Earth: Indian Tales of the Pacific Northwest*. New York: Holt, 1949.

Sakade, Florence. *Japanese Children's Stories*. Rutland, Vermont: Tuttle, 1952.

Sapir, Edward and Harry Hojier, editors. *Navaho Texts*. Iowa City: University of Iowa, 1942.

Sawyer, Ruth. *The Way of the Storyteller*. New York: Viking, 1942, 1962.

Scheer, George P. *Cherokee Animal Tales*. New York: Holiday House, 1968.

Scofield, Elizabeth. *A Fox in One Bite and Other Tasty Tales from Japan*. Palo Alto, California: Kodansha, 1965.

_____. *Hold Tight, Stick Tight: A Collection of Japanese Folk Tales*. Palo Alto, California: Kodansha, 1966.

Sechrist, Elizabeth. *Once in the First Times: Folk Tales from the Philippines*. Philadelphia: Macrae Smith, 1969.

Seki, Keigo. *Folktales of Japan*. Chicago: University of Chicago, 1963.

Seredy, Kate. *The Good Master*. New York: Viking, 1935.

Shedlock, Marie. *The Art of Storytelling*. New York: Dover, 1951.

Stamm, Claus. *The Dumplings and the Demons*. New York: Viking, 1964.

_____. *The Very Special Badgers: A Tale of Magic from Japan*. New York: Viking, 1960.

Stevenson, William. *The Bushbabies*. Boston: Houghton Mifflin, 1965.

Tashjian, Virginia A. *Juba This and Juba That: Story Hour Stretches for Large or Small Groups*. Boston: Little, Brown, 1969.

Tedlock, Dennis. *Finding the Center: Narrative Poetry of the Zuni Indians*. University of Nebraska, 1978.

Thompson, Stith. *Motif-Index of Folk-Literature*. Bloomington and London: Indiana University Press, 1966. 6 vols.

_____. *Tales of the North American Indians*. Bloomington: Indiana University Press, 1966.

Thompson, Vivian Laubach. *Hawaiian Legends of Tricksters and Riddlers.* New York: Holiday House, 1969.

Tooze, Ruth. *The Wonderful Wooden Peacock Flying Machine and Other Tales of Ceylon.* New York: Day, 1969.

Uchida, Yoshiko. *The Magic Listening Cap: More Folk Tales from Japan.* New York: Harcourt Brace, 1955.

Wahl, Jan. *Drakestail.* New York: Greenwillow, 1978.

Walker, Barbara K. *Just Say Hic!* Chicago: Follett, 1965.

Walker, Barbara K. and Warren S. Walker. *Nigerian Folk Tales.* New Brunswick, New Jersey: Rutgers, 1961.

Whitney, Annie Weston and Caroline Canfield Bullock. "Folk-Lore from Maryland" in *Memoirs of the American Folk-Lore Society,* Vol. XVII, 1925.

Wilder, Laura Ingalls. *On the Banks of Plum Creek.* New York: Harper & Row, 1937.

Williams-Ellis, Amabel. *Round the World Fairy Tales.* New York: Warne, 1963.

Withers, Carl. *I Saw a Rocket Walk a Mile: Nonsense Tales, Chants and Songs of Many Lands.* New York: Holt, Rinehart & Winston, 1965.

————. *The Wild Ducks and the Goose.* New York: Holt, Rinehart & Winston, 1968.

Wolkstein, Diane. *The Magic Orange Tree and other Haitian Tales.* New York: Knopf, 1978.

Yoda, Junichi. *The Rolling Rice Ball.* New York: Parents' Magazine Press, 1968.